HOW THE EASTER STORY GREW
FROM GOSPEL TO GOSPEL

Rolland E. Wolfe

HOW THE EASTER STORY GREW FROM GOSPEL TO GOSPEL

Rolland E. Wolfe

The Edwin Mellen Press
Lewiston●Queenston

Wolfe, Rolland E.

How The Easter Story Grew From Gospel To Gospel

ISBN   0-88946-003-5

This book has been registered with the Library of Congress.

CONTENTS

The Easter Problem 1

PART I

THE VALID ACCOUNT OF EASTER OCCURRENCES 7

The Accurate Easter Reporters.. 8

First Easter Report: The Lost Sunrise Dispatch 16

Second Easter Report: Women at the Tomb............................... 20

The Lost Ending to Mark's Original Gospel............................... 25

Third Easter Report: From the Disciples at Midday 28

Fourth Easter Report: Afternoon on the Emmaus Road 31

Fifth Easter Report: Evening in the Emmaus Home 39

Sixth Easter Report: From the Upper Room at Midnight 43

Curtain Call on the First Easter 51

Seventh Easter Report: The Lost Monday Morning Dispatch 54

PART II

WAYS OF ACCOUNTING FOR JESUS' EASTER APPEARANCES.... 61

Resurrection or Immortality? 62

   I.   Physical Death and Bodily Resurrection.......................... 63

  II.   Immortalized and Glorified from the Cross...................... 65

 III.   Jesus Never Died but Invaded and Conquered Hell 70

 IV.   Metaphysical Ghost Appearances or Apparitions 79

  V.   The Easter Appearances were but Optic Illusions 87

 VI.   The Disciples Stole the Body of Jesus........................... 90

VII.   No Death, Only Coma, followed by Physical Revival 92

PART III

HOW THE EASTER STORY GREW FROM GOSPEL TO GOSPEL 105

  I. Growth in the Easter-morning Reporting 106
      1. Change and Expansion in Luke's Rewriting 108
      2. Matthew's Miraclizing of Easter-morning Events 110
      3. The Fourth Gospel's Completely New Version 114
  II. Elaboration in Rewriting the Easter-night Events 120
      1. Mark's Gospel: First Edition 120
      2. Blank-Out in Matthew's Gospel 121
      3. Luke's Salvage of Mark's Easter-night Recording 121
      4. Complete Reconstruction by John 124
      5. Third Meeting with Disciples in Fourth-Gospel
         Appendix 130
      6. Two New Endings to Mark's Gospel 133
  III. The Ultimate Growth Miracle, the Ascension 141
  IV. Easter Growth in New Testament Apocryphal Gospels 154
  V. Continuing Ministry of Jesus in Other Parts of the World 166
      1. Jesus, Mary Magdalene, and Children go to France 166
      2. The Ahmadiyya Story of Christ in India 169
      3. Endless Proliferations on Post-Easter World Ministries 174
  VI. Easter Overshadowed by Pentecost and Passion Observances ... 175
  VII. Valediction on the Miracle of Easter Growth 183

PART IV

GROWTH IN THE MARY STORIES 189

   I.   The Real Mary of the Synoptic Gospels 192

       1.   In the Temple at Twelve 192

       2.   Visit to Jesus' Preaching 194

       3.   Visit Home to Nazareth 197

       4.   The Blessed Womb and Breast? 199

       5.   Mary at Easter and After 199

  II.   Reversal, Revision, and Expansion in the Fourth Gospel 201

 III.   Apocryphizing of Mary in the Passion-Easter Gospels 205

 IV.   Spectacular Forebodings, Death, and Entombment 210

  V.   The Assumption of Mary to Heaven 220

 VI.   Mary Becomes Mother of God and Queen of Heaven 230

VII.   The Challenge of Truth 238

The Easter Problem

The most amazing anomaly regarding "Christian" theology consists in the way it avoids the life and teachings of its founder. The main portion of Christian concern has been focused on the termini of Jesus' life, his birth and death. Even the Apostle's Creed ignores the life, teachings, and religion of Jesus completely as it passes directly from "born of the Virgin Mary" to "suffered under Pontius Pilate." Of even these two pivotal points, the birth and Christmas are overshadowed theologically by the crucifixion and Easter, with attention centered on the resurrection. The days of Jesus' ministry have come to be construed as but the relatively unimportant prelude to the great drama which took place on Easter.

It might be assumed that treatment of Easter would be a simple matter, whose events and significance could be summarized in a few words. Quite the reverse, this is an unbelievably complicated subject. This difficulty is caused largely by the fact that the Easter records present a masterpiece of confused thinking, a mixture of fact, fiction, and theological misconceptions.

One might have supposed that the Easter phenomena would have been considered so significant that they would have been the leading subject throughout the New Testament and

that every book would have made mention of those events.
Here, again, the facts are quite different from what might
have been expected. Only five of the New Testament's
twenty-seven books speak of the events which occurred on
Easter day, with twenty-two being silent on the subject.
Only six of the New Testament's 257 chapters deal with
Easter: two in John and one each in Matthew, Mark, Luke,
and Acts.

What does this amazing silence mean? Did writers of
the epistles and late literature not know what happened on
Easter? Or, did they see no significance in the Easter
events? Possibly those authors disbelieved the spectacular
miracles ascribed to that day and "threw out the baby with
the bath." These are some of the problems that confront one
in approaching an investigation of wnat happened on the
first Easter.

On the question of Easter, people are divided into two
opposing camps. Regrettably, most individuals in each are
totalitarian in their attitude. One group assumes that the
Easter accounts are a hundred percent historically true.
The other regards these narratives as virtually a hundred
percent false. The relatively few who follow a third
approach, the scholarly, find the truth somewhere between
these two extremes.

This study is involved with the changes which take place in preliterary traditions as they are passed on orally over an extensive period of time. Such alteration is caused largely by two factors: (1) the inability of people to pass on material orally without change and elaboration, and (2) the effect which an evolving cult inevitably has in elaborating its traditions.

Since the biblical researcher is confronted here with this dual problem of change and accretion, it is of prime importance to re-evaluate the accounts dealing with the Easter occurrences to see which hold up under discerning scrutiny, and which do not. In this way it is possible to determine, with some degree of certainty, which are the elaborated and mythologized portions of that story. Then the damage in transmission can be reversed by drawing attention away from the accretionary sections and concentrating on those parts which seem assuredly historical.

In such a study the elapse of time between the event and the literary recording is an all important factor. How long was that period of oral transmission? Matthew 2:13-23 states that Jesus was born under the kingship of Herod the Great who died in 4 B.C. If that latest possible date for the birth of Jesus is adopted, the thirty pre-ministerial years in Nazareth (Luke 3:23) bring his emergence into public life to A.D. 26. Since the Synoptic Gospels indicate a one-year ministry, A.D. 27 would seem the most likely year for the crucifixion and the Easter events which followed.

The earliest surviving gospel, Mark, was not produced until almost forty years later at approximately A.D. 65. The best estimates on the other gospels are Luke at A.D. 75, Matthew at A.D. 85, and John at A.D. 100. These datings run into the virtual literary law that the greater the time-span after the event, the greater the measure of inaccuracy, change and fictional elaboration.

In spite of the lateness of even the Marcan and Lucan gospels, it is a delight to report provisionally that the first edition of Mark's gospel displays an almost hundred-percent accuracy and Luke does not lag far behind. These writers attempted to record the Easter events as they occurred. By contrast, Matthew reported Easter as it might have been and John portrayed the Easter story as it should have been. Since the Church follows John as its favorite gospel, and largely avoids Mark and Luke, the following pages will show that much readjustment is needed if the Church proposes to be based on truth.

What occurred on Easter day is not primarily a matter for theologians to determine. Rather, it is an historical problem which can be solved only by carefully examining the relatively few gospel facts that are available. Only after determination has been made as to which items in the record

of that day are historical do theologians have the green
light to proceed with their explanations regarding the
significance of those facts.

No attempt will be made here to review or appraise the
views expressed by the church fathers or summarize what
theologians of the centuries have written. Nor can space be
taken to pass in review what biblical scholars have to offer
on the subject. Here it is proposed to bypass all these
writers and go back to the only ultimate authority, the New
Testament itself. The intent is to make an intensive
re-examination of the gospel records concerning Easter and
its immediate aftermath, to see what they really say
concerning that day which the Church has considered the
greatest in its history.

By means of such an approach one is able to observe how
the nucleus of historical truth has become almost lost under
the avalanche of later additions that usually are far more
spectacular and abounding in miracles. In short, it is
possible to see how the story has grown in moving from
gospel to gospel as the Easter tapestry became woven, thread
by thread.

This book has been written for those discerning people
who like their religion to be based on truth rather than on
falsehood and fancy. Its pages proceed on the assumption
that truth should be welcomed in religion as well as in the

sciences, and that only as religion becomes more truthful does it hold much chance of maintaining influence in the years ahead. It would seem that the reappraisal of Easter day is the one area, above all places, where Christians should exercise that option.

The following chapters are written in nontechnical language so they can be understood by the common reader. Scripture passages are indicated rather continuously for facility in checking the judgments expressed. The translations are the author's own renditions.

The author is deeply indebted to the vast body of biblical scholarship which has made this study possible. For assistance in tracing continuing growth of the Easter story in the non-canonical gospels, chief indebtedness has been to the superb work of Montague R. James, the first English scholar to do definitive work in the New Testament apocryphal writings. He collected those documents and published them in his Apocryphal New Testament. Special thanks are due the Oxford University Press for making extensive quotations from that volume possible.

PART I

THE VALID ACCOUNT OF EASTER OCCURRENCES

The Accurate Easter Reporters

As a prelude to deciding where the Easter stories stand on the scale of validity, it is desirable to cast the spotlight of attention upon the people most intimately involved in the events of Easter morning. It is needful to see how they recovered the information of that day and mediated it to the Church through the gospel record.

Although each of the four gospels presents a description of the first Easter, the following pages will show that the entire authentic reporting of the first Easter in the New Testament presumably comes from a mother and her son. Therefore, it is fitting to begin this quest by introducing this key pair of reporters and appraising their competence to record the Easter events. Since the mother probably was the more knowledgeable of the two, she may well be introduced first.

That mother was none other than Mary Magdalene who supposedly had been a notorious prostitute. Upon coming in contact with the spirit of Jesus she at once became attracted to it. In light of Luke 8:2 it is fairly certain that the words leading up to it in the final verses of chapter 7 describe the strategic episode in her transformation from being a big-operating woman of the streets to becoming a devoted follower of Jesus.

"And lo, a woman who was in the city, a sinner: and
when she learned that he was reclining at dinner in the
Pharisee's house, she brought an alabaster flask of
ointment, and standing behind at his feet, weeping, she
proceeded to bathe his feet with her tears, wipe them with
the hair of her head, and kiss his feet, and anoint them
with the ointment. Now when the Pharisee who had invited
him saw it, he spoke to himself, saying, 'If this man were a
prophet he would have perceived who and what manner of woman
this is who touched him, that she is a sinner.' And Jesus
answering said to him . . . 'Her sins, which have been many,
are forgiven, for she loved much.' . . . And he said to the
woman, 'Your faith has saved you. Go in peace'" (Luke
7:36-50). Mary Magdalene's dramatic action on that occasion
shows her remorse over her past ways and joy over the new
redeemed life Jesus had brought to her.

This new convert proceeded at once to gather together a
group of women followers and organized them into a women's
auxiliary to Jesus' movement. "And with him were the
twelve, and certain women who had been healed of evil
spirits and infirmities: Mary who was called Magdalene,
from whom seven demons had gone out, and Joanna the wife of
Chuzas, Herod's steward, and Susanna, and many others who
provided for them from their resources" (Luke 8:1-3).

As this development occurred near the beginning of his ministry, it is apparent that Mary Magdalene was an eyewitness thereafter of most events in Jesus' ministry. Her name occurs fourteen times in the gospels and is referred to as the woman from whom Jesus cast out "seven demons" (Mark 16:9).

Since the disciples vanished immediately after Jesus' arrest in Gethsemane, Mary Magdalene and her women associates were the only ones of Jesus' followers who kept near the action and were present as observers at the crucifixion. "And there also were women beholding from afar, among whom were both Mary Magdalene, and Mary, the mother of James the younger and of Joses, and Salome; who, when he was in Galilee, followed him and ministered unto him, and many other women who came up with him to Jerusalem" (Mark 15:40-41).

Mary Magdalene also observed the entombment and made preparations to anoint the body. With her associates she came early to the tomb on Easter morning, "And Mary Magdalene and Mary the mother of Joses observed where he was laid. And when the Sabbath was past, Mary Magdalene, and Mary the mother of Joses, and Salome bought spices that they might come and anoint him" (Mark 15:47-16:1).

First mention of Mary Magdalene in each instance shows that she was the recognized leader of the women followers on

Good Friday, Saturday, and Easter morning. During Easter
day she, apparently, gathered the fleeing disciples
together. The notable meeting that evening of the eleven
and others, when Jesus came and was present with them,
presumably took place in her rented quarters (Luke 24:33).
It may well be that the Last Supper had been held in her
"upper room." The pentecostal experience, as described in
Acts 2, probably occurred also in that same upper room.
Well on, into the Book of Acts, this "house of Mary"
continued as the headquarters of the Church (Acts 12:12).

From the foregoing references it becomes apparent that
Mary Magdalene was "the leader" of the incipient Jerusalem
church. This was particularly true from Good Friday to
Easter when the disciples had become immobilized and faded
out of the picture. During those closing days of Holy Week,
probably the most strategic in Christian history, Mary
Magdalene was the person who was most knowledgeable
regarding what transpired on Easter day.

The other member of the reporting pair, Mary
Magdalene's close associate in observing and recording the
Easter phenomena, was her son who bore the name John Mark.
Acts 12:12 gives the information that Mark's mother was
named Mary. Then the question becomes, which Mary? Since
the other Mary in the Easter observances is listed as "Mary,
the mother of Joses" or "Mary the mother of James" (Mark

15:47; 16:1), it leaves Mary Magdalene as the "Mary, the mother of John whose surname was Mark" (Acts 12:12).

Apparently Mark was the illegitimate son of Mary Magdalene's preconversion days. He may well have been at her side during much of Jesus' ministry. Likely he was the lad with the five barley loaves and the two fishes at the time of feeding the multitude (John 6:9).

Since the home of Mary and Mark, within the walled city of Jerusalem, presumably had been the site of the Last Supper, the Easter evening gathering, and headquarters of the very early church, that structure became immortalized. Since Mark probably survived his mother, and in a man's world, that building eventually came to be called by the son's name as the Monastery of Saint Mark. Its "upper room" continues today to be revered as the place where the communion was instituted. Foot-washing also continues to be observed there on Thursday evening of every Holy Week on that presumed same spot where John represents that rite as having taken place.

As the likely attendant at the Last Supper, Mark was probably the only non-disciple who had the privilege of observing everything that went on and hearing all that was said at that historic meal. After Jesus and the disciples had left for the Garden of Gethsemane, following the

supper, Mark probably put the room in order and then retired
for the night.

Before getting asleep he likely sensed commotion
outside, and heard someone say that an arresting party was
going to get Jesus. Knowing that he and the disciples were
going to the Garden of Gethsemane, Mark resolved to go at
once and warn him. Witout taking time to dress, and with
only a nightcloth around himself, this young lad appears to
have rushed out of the city and across tne Kidron Valley to
the garden.

Mark arrived at Gethsemane about the same time as the
soldiers -- too late to warn Jesus. After the disciples all
had taken to their heels and ran, Mark remained with Jesus.
When the arresting party grabbed this youth, he slipped out
of the nightcloth and fled naked to his home within the
walled city of Jerusalem.

Mark described that rather naive happening at the time
of Jesus' arrest in an anonymous manner. "And a certain
young man followed with him, having a linen cloth thrown
about him over his naked body, and they laid hold on him but
he left the linen cloth and fled naked" (Mark 14:51-52).
This "young man" presumably was John Mark, the gospel
writer, who in his typical modesty refrained from giving his
name.

If someone else had been the one involved in such an otherwise insignificant happening, it would hardly have merited a place in the record. However, since he came so close to being arrested with Jesus, that incident meant much to Mark. The essential point here is that he was the last of Jesus' followers to be with him at the end of Holy Week. It will be seen that this "young man" also was probably the most complete observer of the events on Easter day.

Mark was fitted further for writing his gospel by his intimate and extensive contacts with the pillars of the early Christian movement. He was the nephew, as Colossians 4:10 probably should be translated, of Barnabas, who presumably was Mary Magdalene's brother. Barnabas was the first important foreign missionary of the Church. Mark was present at least part of that notable year of preaching at Antioch when Barnabas salvaged Paul into an effective apostleship. Mark was therefore appropriately chosen to accompany Barnabas and Paul on their first joint missionary adventure (Acts 12:25; 13:5, 13).

When Paul refused to take Mark on the second trip, Barnabas broke with Paul, and took his nephew with him on his own missionary journey to Cyprus (Acts 15:37-39). Mark later reintegrated himself into the Pauline circle and was part of their extensive activities (Colossians 4:10; II Timothy 4:11; Philemon 24). Early-church tradition asserts

that Mark also was with Peter on some of that apostle's
evangelistic campaigns. All this shows how intimately Mark
was involved in the inner circle of those who built the
Christian Church.

Mark's intimate contacts with his mother, the other
women, the disciples, Jesus, and the apostles of the Early
Church, gave him an unusual opportunity to write
authoritatively. The resultant gospel may be viewed as a
joint production of Mary Magdalene and her son. A
substantial part of it presumably consists of her
recollections of episodes in the life of Jesus. These
accounts are supplemented by Mark's own observations,
particularly at Easter where at times he was the only
observer. Since he probably outlived her and since it was a
man's world, this gospel which they jointly produced came to
bear only the son's name.

In approaching a study of Easter day, the spotlight of
attention must be focused on Mark's gospel. As the earliest
surviving gospel, it had the advantage of being produced
nearest to the events it was describing, before memories
faded and spurious modifications intruded themselves. Since
none of the eleven disciples ever wrote a gospel, Mark and
his mother were left as the only authors who were present on
Easter day and saw what had occurred. Even Mary Magdalene
had to take second place here for it will be shown that her

son saw more of the Easter events than did she. In fact, he saw more than any other individual. It also will be shown that the first edition of Mark's gospel contained perhaps all the valid information that was salvaged from the Easter occurrences. All these advantages, especially the fact of its being the only gospel containing firsthand observations of the dramatic events on that momentous day, leaves Mark's gospel as the only Easter record that approaches hundred-percent validity.

First Easter Report: The Lost Sunrise Dispatch

Since Easter was such an important day, that in its significance has come to be thought of by many as over-shadowing the entire ministry of Jesus, one would have expected detailed reports of what occurred on that notable day. To one's surprise, the opposite is true. It is to be regretted that none of the gospels, or even all four combined, contain any semblance of a complete account concerning what took place in Jerusalem on that occasion which, for Christians, is the most important of all days.

The best that can be done is to focus attention on the five apparently authentic reports that came from various hours of that day and the ensuing night. These are the only available sources of information from which to reconstruct the history of that first Easter day. It therefore is

necessary to make the most use of these successive
dispatches that have been preserved by Mark and Luke.

It becomes evident at once that the earliest record of
Easter-morning occurrences has either been lost or has been
excised from Mark's gospel. To be more specific, the
initial and most important block of information about what
happened between chapters 15 and 16 of Mark is missing.

That lost material must have answered a galaxy of
queries. Who came to the tomb first on Easter morning? Did
that person hear Jesus call for help from the tomb? Who
rolled away the stone from tne door of the tomb? Was Jesus
still bound in the grave clothes? Did this individual
proceed to unwind Jesus? In what physical condition did he
appear? What did ne do for clothing? Why was he impatient
to leave the tomb area? Why did he not go at once to the
upper room and confer with Mary Magdalene and the
disciples? Why, instead, did he strike out at once for
Galilee? Did he start out without food? Did he appear
badly emaciated? What else did he say in addition to
stating that he was returning to Galilee?

These are the types of questions which one might assume
that Mark must have answered in the first part of his Easter
report. This study has been driven to the conclusion that
such a block of material originally was present in his
gospel but has been removed, presumably because of not being

sufficiently miraculous. The first task in approaching the
Easter story is to attempt a hypothetical reconstruction of
what may have been contained in that lost or expurgated
earliest block of material.

At breakfast, Mark's mother, Mary Magdalene,
undoubtedly would have told how she and two of the other
women were going to the tomb to anoint the body of Jesus.
Following that meal, Mary Magdalene presumably left the
house to pick up Salome and Mary, the mother of Jacob, at
the respective places where they were staying.

After his mother had departed, Mark seems to have
decided that he too would like to see what the situation in
the tomb was like. So he rushed out of the house and
proceeded to the place of burial, apparently some distace
away from the populated areas of the city, arriving there
before the women.

Upon approaching the tomb Mark must have been surprised
to see that the stone had been rolled away from the tomb
entrance. Apparently he found someone present at the tomb.
This clearly was not Jesus. But, who was it? To find the
answer one must search the Good-Friday account.

The best guess is that the Roman centurion who was last
with Jesus at the crucifixion may also have been first at
the tomb on Easter morning, since he was in charge of
guarding the crucifixion and grave areas. This was the

centurion who, so impressed by the way Jesus bore his
sufferings on the cross, became certain that Jesus was an
innocent person and that a great injustice had been done.
According to Mark this centurion said, if translated
properly, "Surely this man was a son of God," i.e., "a godly
man" (Mark 15:39). Resolving the idiom, Luke paraphrased by
saying, "And when the centurion saw what was done he
glorified God, saying, 'Certainly this was a righteous man'"
(Luke 23:47).

Something like the following reconstruction seems
necessary. Because of his high regard for Jesus, this guard
may well have given special attention to the tomb into which
this victim had been placed. Upon making his rounds very
early on that Sunday morning he presumably heard calls for
help when he came by that tomb.

As Joseph of Arimathea had rolled the stone to close
the tomb's door (Mark 15:46), the centurion now rolled the
stone away. Inside the tomb he found Jesus alive, but bound
tightly within the cocoon-like grave wrappings of linen
cloth (Luke 23:53). First move in the rescue consisted in
unwinding those restraining "grave-clothes." Then the
centurion likely provided garments or helped Jesus fashion a
semblance of clothing from the linen wrappings. With a
feeling of urgency, Jesus left the tomb area at once. He
made only one request of the centurion, that he tell any

disciples who might come that he was leaving at once for Galilee and would meet them there (Mark 16:7).

The centurion must have remained dutifully at the tomb until someone from Jesus' group should arrive. Mark happened to be that person, coming soon after Jesus had left for his journey northward. Thereupon the centurion relayed to Mark the message with which Jesus had entrusted him. With that obligation taken care of, the centurion likely proceeded on his further rounds of duty. Left alone, Mark evidently entered the tomb to examine more carefully the place where Jesus had lain and what remained of his grave wrappings.

Second Easter Report: Women at the Tomb

The second Easter report, concerning the three women who visited the tomb with intent to anoint the dead body of Jesus, has survived in Mark 16:1-8. Although it is gratifying to find these eight authentic verses, it is regrettable that only such a small number are devoted to Easter morning. Moreover, of these eight verses, four (1-3 and 8) tell of the coming and going of the women, their plans and reactions. These verses, with their feminine interests, reflect Mary Magdalene's part in the gospel authorship. To Mary Magdalene the trip to and from the tomb meant much, but those four verses are virtually irrelevant to the basic Easter story.

This disproportion leaves only four terse verses to describe what the women found at the tomb. This lack of information regarding such a strategic occurrence is absurd. Nevertheless, in the absence of anything better, we must be resigned to this fragmentary nature of the first authentic Easter material and must make the best of it.

"And when the Sabbath was past, Mary Magdalene, and Mary the mother of Jacob, and Salome, bought spices, that they might come and anoint him. And very early, on the first day of the week, they came to the tomb when the sun was risen. And they were saying among themselves, 'Who will roll the stone away from the door of the tomb for us?' And looking up, they saw that the stone had been rolled back, for it was very large. And entering into the tomb they saw a young man sitting on the right side, clothed in a white garment, and they were amazed" (Mark 16:1-5).

At that point Mark relayed to the women the message as given to him by the presumed centurion. "And he said to them, 'Do not be amazed. You seek Jesus, the Nazarene, who has been crucified. He has risen. He is not here. Behold the place where they laid him. But go, tell his disciples, and Peter, he is going before you into Galilee. There you shall see him as he said unto you'" (Mark 16:6-7).

Verses 4 to 7 record how the women were startled by what they saw upon coming to the tomb. First, their concern over how they could remove the large stone from the door was taken care of when they saw that it already had been rolled back.

Second, upon entering the tomb they were "amazed" at what they found. They expected to see the body of Jesus, but instead "saw a young man sitting on the right side, clothed in a white garment." Who was this "young man?" The key to that identification is found in Mark 14:51-52.

Earlier in "The Accurate Easter Reporters" it was seen that when almost arrested with Jesus on Maundy Thursday evening, Mark described himself anonymously as "a certain young man." On Easter morning, in the tomb, he is identified similarly as "a young man." In both instances the dress is indicated: "a linen cloth thrown about him over his naked body" in Mark 15:51 and "clothed in a white garment" in Mark 16:5. These similar designations serve to identify Mark as not only the last to have been with Jesus before his arrest and crucifixion but also the first of nis followers to arrive at the tomb on Easter morning.

An objection to this unidentified "young man" having been Mark is that he did not speak with such words as would have been expected from him. Of himself Mark would not have used the formal words, "you seek Jesus, the Nazarene, who has been crucified" (Mark 16:6). However, in addressing the women Mark seems to have been repeating the words of the centurion, passing them on to the women exactly as they had been spoken to Mark in the first instance.

In addition to Mark's quoting the nonintimate and strange statement of the supposed centurion, four other factors contributed to the women, even Mary Magdalene, not recognizing her son when in that tomb. (1) Since Mark likely had been left at home that morning, to see him in the tomb would not have been within range of the women's expectations. (2) As they came from the bright sunshine of the outside suddenly into the relative darkness of a tomb, it would have been possible for them to discern in it only the vaguest of shapes and colors. As they apparently were in that tomb only a few seconds, they bolted out before their eyes had sufficient time to make adjustment. It therefore is doubtful if the women saw the speaker with any distinctness. (3) The sound-changing abilities of tomb chambers with their reverberations and echoes, distort voices to the point of unnaturalness. (4) As suggested by Mark 16:8, the women were so excited at hearing the astounding news, and finding the body gone, that they scarcely heard what the speaker was saying and were therefore in no shape to form any proper judgment as to whom they were hearing. In light of these four explanations it

becomes understandable how it could have been possible that
Mary Magdalene, and the other women, did not recognize her
son under tnose circumstances.

The author of the present book can understand how such
a failure to recognize a member of the family could be
possible since he once had a comparable experience at a time
of great excitement. In the dusk of late evening, while
lost in a Virginia woods, he failed to recognize even his
own son upon encountering him, although he was speaking and
only a few feet away. Mary Magdalene's failure to recognize
her son in the darkness of the tomb, with its distorting
acoustical reverberations, was likely no more remarkable.

Why did Mark not say plainly that he was the "young
man" in the tomb when the women arrived? The answer is that
Mark appears to have been overly modest with regard to
mentioning himself in his gospel and therefore his name
never occurs.

In addition to the three unexpected signs that morning
(stone rolled away, the body of Jesus gone, and a young man
seated in the tomb), a fourth surprise consisted in what the
women heard. That message presumably had been given by
Jesus to the centurion who relayed it to Mark who further
relayed it to these three women. Jesus stated that he was
going to Galilee immediately and would meet his disciples
there. In that more hospitable nomeland, where the

multitudes of receptive followers were waiting, he would
resume his ministry, away from annoyance by the Jerusalem
religious hierarchy.

This second Easter-morning dispatch, the only one that
survives in our gospels, ends in a strangely abrupt manner
as it tells how the three women "went out, and fled from the
tomb, for trembling and astonishment had overcome them, and
they said nothing to anyone, for they were terrified" (Mark
16:8).

The Lost Ending to Mark's Original Gospel

Manuscript research yields the observation that the
most ancient remaining manuscripts of Mark's gospel end with
16:8. This is the ending in the two great authoritative
Greek uncial codices, the Sinaitic and Vatican Manuscripts.
Following verse 8 the Sinaitic Manuscript, the most
authentic of all, has left a column blank, presumably for
copying the lost original ending if it should ever appear.
As one of three endings, the Greek uncial Codex Regius (L)
also witnesses to this original ending of the gospel at
verse 8. Cursive 22 has this truncated form as one of two
endings, with a note. This short form is found also in the
Sinaitic Syriac, the best manuscripts of the Armenian, and
some of the older Ethiopic manuscripts. It is implicit in
manuscript k of the Old Latin and in the margin of the

Heracleian Syriac. This form, without the ending in verses 9-20, was assumed to be most original by the church historian Eusebius, Jerome, Victor of Antioch, and the writer of the "Oration on the Resurrection."[1]

In spite of this unanimous evidence as to the ending of Mark's gospel in all extant early manuscripts, even a superficial glance suggests that verse 8 could not have been a gospel ending. "They said nothing to anyone, for they were terrified" leaves the story up in the air in a way that no gospel writer would have done. The inevitable conclusion is that the original ending has been removed from this gospel.

This excision of Mark's original ending probably was made because his continuing account of Easter happenings was not sufficiently miraculous to satisfy the theologians of the Early Church. Therefore they eliminated it, leaving but a truncated gospel. This deletion must have been made very early, possibly when only the original manuscript existed.

Some later individual, realizing that this gospel with the expurgated ending was not complete, did the further indignity of appending a more spectacular, but spurious, false ending to the gospel as 16:9-20.

Since Mark was a valid reporter, loss of his gospel's ending would seem to be one of the major literary losses of Christian history. As it is, the gospel breaks off at

perhaps 7:00 a.m. on Easter day. If only we had Mark's
version as to what occurred on the remainder of that day and
what happened to Jesus immediately thereafter! As almost
two millennia have passed since that loss, there is not much
hope that the lost ending will ever be recovered in any
archaeological excavation.

However, reconstructing the further events of that
first Easter forenoon, afternoon, and evening is not so
hopeless as the loss of Mark's gospel ending might suggest.
This is where Luke came into the picture to save the day.
That writer, approximately a decade after Mark, combining
the Q Gospel (later lost, of Jesus' teachings) and the
Gospel of Mark (with its life and ministry of Jesus) to form
the complete Gospel of Luke.

Luke appears to have used an original edition of Mark's
gospel, before the genuine ending was cut off. Luke began
his report of Easter by copying the early-morning record
from Mark 16:1-8, although abbreviating somewhat and making
several changes. He evidently then went on to transcribe
the remainder of Mark's original ending. There is no reason
to believe that, in describing that momentous day's events,
Luke had any other material, from his own researches, to
contribute.

Since Mark's description of that day bears practically
a hundred-percent stamp of accuracy, and since Luke usually

is almost as reliable a reporter, it may be assumed that his transcribings of the day's later events also were largely reliable. The Church stands highly indebted to Luke for having preserved Mark's record of the continuing events of that most significant day. The Marcan-Lucan recording should be treasured as containing perhaps the only existent valid facts regarding the forenoon, afternoon, and evening of the first Easter day.

Third Easter Report: From the Disciples at Midday

Before turning to Luke's salvaging of Mark's record of Easter forenoon, it is desirable to reconstruct hypothetically what the three women did and thought during the several hours between leaving the tomb in fright and the time Luke's resumption of Mark's account continues.

After returning probably to the home of Mary Magdalene, the women likely thought things over in the quiet seclusion of those domestic surroundings. There they undoubtedly made the most of their opportunity by securing detailed information from Mark, when he arrived home, as to what exactly had occurred at the tomb.

Mark must have told the women about his meeting the centurion at the tomb and his telling of rolling the stone away, liberating Jesus from his bound condition, outfitting him for road travel, the message left by Jesus for the disciples, and how he left quickly for Galilee.

Because of not having seen Jesus, Mark was unable to say anything about Jesus' physical condition and how he looked. Nevertheless, by answering such inquiries as he was able, Mark must have proved to be the women's magical informer. At that forenoon hour it may be that the centurion, the three women, and Mark were the only individuals in Jerusalem who knew about the empty tomb and that Jesus was alive.

Eventually the curiosities of the women probably became pretty well satisfied. Also, their surprise, excitement, and fright became worn off somewhat. By that time these women apparently felt moved to desist from their first impulse, which was to say "nothing to anyone" (Mark 16:8) about their experiences and observations that morning at the sepulchre.

Someone in the group may well have suggested that they should search for the disciples and inform them concerning what had been discovered at the tomb. As this counsel seemed wise, the women "told all these things to the eleven, and to all the others . . . But these words appeared in their sight as idle talk, and they disbelieved them" (Luke 24:9, 11).

What phase of the women's story did the disciples discount as pure fancy? Was it the report of the empty tomb? Were they devastated by puzzlement over what had

happened to the body of Jesus? Rumors of his being alive
again must have seemed as the ultimate idiocy.

Because the disciples were engulfed in an instant with
this avalanche of incomprehensibles, their credability lag
forced them to deny the truthfulness of all of it. How
could they believe these hearsay reports when neither Mark
nor any of the women had seen Jesus and the word that he was
alive rested only on the word of a perhaps lying Roman
soldier? Consequently, the disciples dismissed what the
women had said about Jesus being alive as but "idle talk"
and they "disbelieved."

Undismayed by this lack of response from the disciples,
the women urged the eleven to go and see the empty tomb in
an effort to prove that their words were not "idle talk."
Neither Mark's gospel nor the original text of Luke show any
response on the part of the ten disciples who did not show
enough interest to visit the tomb and see.

By contrast, Luke states that Peter finally was
persuaded to visit the tomb. "But Peter arose and ran to
the tomb and, stooping and looking in, he saw the linen
clothes by themselves, and he departed to his home,
perplexed over that which had come to pass" (Luke 24:12).

Even Peter did not show enough interest to enter the
tomb, examine the remaining grave clothes, and observe where
Jesus had lain. He only "stooped" and "looked in."
Although Peter saw the empty tomb, this rock disciple

remained "perplexed," which probably means he could not believe that Jesus was alive. Here the curtain is drawn on Luke's presumably authentic fragment salvaged from Mark's record of Easter at midday.

Fourth Easter Report: Afternoon on the Emmaus Road

The fourth report on the events of Easter day came from two admirers of Jesus who had spent Easter day in Jerusalem and were returning home. "And behold, two of them were going that very day to a village named Emmaus, which was threescore furlongs from Jerusalem. And they conversed with each other concerning all these things which had happened" (Luke 24:13-14).

The identity of Emmaus presents a problem. The modern village by that name, Emwas, is some fifteen miles northwest of Jerusalem as the crow flies. Another Emmaus, now in ruins, on the same road, was only approximately five miles distant. The Greek text says Emmaus was sixty stadia (furlongs) from Jerusalem. With eight stadia to the mile, Luke was stating the distance as seven and a half miles. In light of the probable weakened condition of Jesus from his crucifixion experience, and that he made this round trip during the afternoon and evening, the nearer village, with round trip of ten miles, would seem indicated. Luke evidently exaggerated the mileage somewhat.

As the two were nearing their home town they overtook
Jesus, who walked with them the remainder of the way. "And
it came to pass, while they conversed and questioned
together, that Jesus himself drew near and went with them.
However, their eyes were so dull that they did not recognize
him. And he said to them, 'What conversations are these
which you are having with each other while you are
walking?' And they stood still -- looking sad. Then the
one of them named Cleopas answering said to him, 'Do you
alone sojourn in Jerusalem and not know the things which
have come to pass there in these days?' And he said to
them, 'What things?' And they said to him, 'The things
concerning Jesus, the Nazarene, who was a prophet mighty in
deed and word before God and all the people, and how the
chief priests and our rulers delivered him up to be
condemned to death, and crucified him. But we had hoped
that he was the one who should liberate Israel. Moreover,
and besides all this, it is now the third day since these
things came to pass'" (Luke 24:15-21).

As these two men informed their walking companion that
Jesus was a prophet and of the details leading to his trial
and death by crucifixion, it was indeed the ultimate in
"carrying coals to Newcastle."

Although it may be assumed that the Emmaus men's
account is correct, it nevertheless throws itself open to

diametrically opposite interpretations. The most natural
deduction would be that, between the time Peter went to the
tomb on Easter forenoon and the time the two from Emmaus
left for home in the afternoon, news about the empty tomb
and Jesus being alive had spread all over Jerusalem. This
might seem to be indicated by the surprise of the two men
that any one could be in Jerusalem and not know about what
had gone on there "in these days" (Luke 24:18).

However, closer examination of the roadway conversation
reveals that nothing is said in verses 15-21 about any
resurrection. Up to that point the two from Emmaus were
talking only about the crucifixion of Jesus.

Passover that year occurred on the Sabbath. Since the
crucifixion had taken place so near the start of the
Sabbath, which began at approximately 6:00 p.m. on Friday
evening, most of the people in the city had been frantically
occupied with Passover preparations on that Friday afternoon
when the tragic deed was performed on Calvary. Even the
devoted women-followers did not have time to anoint the body
that evening.

In light of the normal restrictions on Sabbath travel,
and complete absorption with the Passover rituals and
following festivities, there was little opportunity for news
to spread during the Sabbath period from 6:00 p.m. Friday
evening to 6:00 p.m. Saturday evening. Then followed
Saturday night.

The news of Jesus' crucifixion consequently did not have opportunity to spread over Jerusalem until the Sabbath and its following night were over. This means that the tragedy on Calvary did not dawn upon the consciousness of that city, and become a subject of general conversation, until on the first day of the week, which is now styled as Easter day. If looked at properly, the conversation of the two men would seem to confirm this, that the excitement in Jerusalem, among the admiring populace that day, was when they learned that Jesus had been given final trial, crucifixion, and entombment in quick succession at a time when the attention of most Jerusalemites was distracted to Passover preparation.

One statement by these men reveals the thoughts of the masses on Easter day regarding the role of Jesus: "But we had hoped that he was the one who would liberate Israel" (Luke 24:21). The fires of revolution had been kindled on Palm Sunday morning when, according to Luke's minority report (Luke 19:35-44), the disciples "set Jesus" on the donkey (vs. 35) and forcibly paraded him into Jerusalem as the new King of Israel who would drive the Romans out of Palestine and liberate their country. Luke tells further how Jesus' "disciples" shouted "with a loud voice" saying, "Blessed is the king who comes in the name of the Lord" (vss. 37-38). This manifesto inflamed the suppressed masses who joined in welcoming the new King. Mark records them as shouting, "Blessed be the coming kingdom of our father David" (Mark 11:10).

Luke records that Jesus was so mortified over this disgraceful entry into Jerusalem that he wept over the way the populace, and even the disciples, could think of him only as a political figure, a king who would raise armies and drive out the Romans, rather than a religious reformer who would bring new spiritual life to the Holy City. Because of that shortsightedness he felt certain that Jerusalem and the temple would be destroyed, with not one stone left upon another (Luke 19:41-44).

Jesus probably explained further to these two men how wrong they, the Jerusalem populace, and even the disciples were in being swept off their feet by the monumental misconception of Holy Week that he would be the political Messiah who would win for Israel independence from Rome and set up his own government. He had no aspirations to become the Hebrew Messiah (anointed), or Christ (anointed) in Greek. These were but underground terms for king, anointing being the ritual by which a king was inducted into office. Jesus must have stressed to his walking companions that his was a spiritual mission and not a political role. He had wanted to be only a humble teacher and prophet.

The conversation of the two men on the Emmaus Road shows that the Palm Sunday hope, of Jesus' becoming king, was replaced in the minds of the populace with Easter despair over the shattering of their expectations.

Following their telling of the general concern in Jerusalem on that first Easter afternoon over the crucifixion, the two men went on to describe the events of that day insofar as they concerned the company of Jesus' followers. "Moreover, certain women of our company amazed us, having been early at the tomb; and when they found not his body, they came saying that they had seen also a vision of angels who said that he was alive; and certain of those who were with us went to the tomb and found it just as the women had said, but they did not see him" (Luke 24:22-24). These men added to the Easter information by reporting that during the afternoon others of the inner circle visited the tomb, following the example of Peter who did so during the forenoon.

In response to the interest of his walking companions, Jesus then explained to these men of Emmaus that his death in Jerusalem had been inevitable (Luke 24:25-26). "And he said to them, 'Oh, inapprehensive men and slow of mind to believe in all that the prophets have spoken! Was it not necessary for him to suffer these things and to enter into his glory?'"

Since Jesus did not conceive of himself as Christ, it is evident that a mistake has taken place in transcribing

Luke's gospel at this point. Therefore, as indicated in the
foregoing translation of Luke 24:26, Jesus probably said
"Was it not necessary for him to suffer these things . . .?"
rather than "Was it not nessary for the Christ to suffer
these things . . .?"

If he should come to Jerusalem, and try to put
spiritual life into the narrow forms of fossilized religion
practiced there, it would likely mean persecution,
suffering, or even death. As will be pointed out under
CURTAIN CALL, he had given the same warning to the disciples
many times concerning the danger of such an eventuality if
they should do their religious duty.

That afternoon roadway conversation came to a climax as
Jesus favored those two men with more specific explanations
of the Scriptures. "And, beginning from Moses and from all
the prophets, he interpreted to them in all the Scriptures
the sayings concerning himself" (Luke 24:27). What
interpretations did he give? As these are not stated, we
are left to try and reconstruct what he may have said on
that occasion regarding the Scriptures and himself.

Since it is said that Jesus began with Moses,
Deuteronomy 18:15, 18 probably was quoted, with the words
applied to himself. "Yahweh, your god, will raise up unto
you from your midst, of your brethren, a prophet like unto
me; to him you shall listed . . . And Yahweh said, . . . 'I

will put my words in his mouth, and he shall speak to them all that I shall command him.'"

Since Jesus then possibly led up to the inevitability of his recent crucifixion, the next turn of his communications may well have been along the line of what he had said earlier: "Therefore also the wisdom of God said, 'I will send unto them prophets and apostles, and some of them they will kill and persecute, that the blood of all the prophets, which was shed from the foundation of the world, may be required of this generation, from the blood of Abel unto the blood of Zachariah who perished between the altar and the sanctuary: I say to you it shall indeed be required of this generation'" (Luke 11:49-51).

Jesus probably repeated to these men also the words of his lament over Jerusalem (Luke 13:33-34) when he said, ". . . it cannot be that a prophet should perish except in Jerusalem. O Jerusalem, Jerusalem, that kills the prophets and stones those who are sent to her! How often would I have gathered your children together, even as a hen her own brood under her wings, but you would not!"

It is clear from these passages that Jesus considered himself to be a prophet, and Jerusalem was the city that killed the prophets. He could well know from Scripture, if history should repeat itself, that it was likely to mean death for himself as well if he should try to minister in that city of reactionary religion.

By now the day was "far spent" and the three travelers were nearing the village in which two of them lived. The Emmaus pair must have marveled at the facility of their walking companion in explaining the Scriptures. What a privilege these two men enjoyed to spend those moments of intimacy in company with the matchless one but how little they comprehended of its opportunity and significance!

Fifth Easter Report: Evening in the Emmaus Home

What was Jesus doing on that Emmaus Road when Mark 16:7 says Galilee was his destination? One would have expected him to take the main highway north from Jerusalem, through Shechem and Samaria, to Nazareth.

By detouring through Emmaus, northwest from Jerusalem, he probably was thinking to elude any authorities or other people who might go in search of him. From Emmaus only zigzag byways led through the Hill Country of Ephraim toward the north. He apparently decided on returning to Galilee by those little-traveled roads on which he was not likely to be recognized and be returned to Jerusalem forcibly.

The record of Jesus' arrival in Emmaus is as follows: "And they drew near unto the village to which they were going, but he made as though he would go farther. However, they prevailed upon him, saying, 'Lodge with us, for it is toward evening, and the day is now far gone.' So he went in to lodge with them" (Luke 24:28-29).

Jesus apparently wanted to press on farther before stopping for the night. Although he evidently had shown remarkable powers of resistance on the previous three days, he found himself unable to hold out against the insistence of these two men that he share their hospitality.

It usually has been taken for granted that Jesus sat down to eat at a table with these men as soon as they entered the house. However, this assumption is subject to question. Since a Palestinian host usually takes considerable time to prepare food worthy of a guest, Jesus likely was in that Emmaus house for several hours or more before the evening meal was served. At that time, from when the day was "far gone" until presumably after dark when the food became ready, was undoubtedly spent in conversation. If only we had a recording of that interchange, which probably continued the trends set by the roadway conversation of the afternoon!

Luke then went on to describe what transpired when the evening meal finally was served. "And it came to pass, when he had reclined at meat with them, he took the loaf and blessed; and breaking it, he gave to them. Then their eyes were opened and they recognized him" (Luke 24:30-31).

The great companion illusion because "breaking bread" is mentioned, is that Jesus administered communion to the two men on that occasion. To understand this scene one must know something about the Ortnodox Jewish meal through the centuries. Even today the beginning of the Orthodox meal consists of each person taking in their hands the piece of bread which has been put at their place, breaking it in two and at the same time asking God's blessing upon the oread and the meal which it initiates. Each individual becomes seated after the blessing and then proceeds to eat the broken bread with the rest of the meal. In that poor Emmaus home, with no table or chairs, the procedure was varied to the extent of reclining on the floor.

The oiggest irregularity in the Emmaus meal was that Jesus evidently refrained from eating. Instead, he gave his broken bread to the two men, presumably offering one piece to the host on his right and the other to the host on his left. This could not be called a "communion" since no wine entered into the picture.

Tnere presumably was nothing in the ritual of oreaking and blessing the bread that was notable. However, there must have oeen something distinctive in Jesus' remarks to those men as he gave the two pieces of broken bread to them. Consequently, they suddenly realized wno he was as ". . . their eyes were opened and they recognized him" in tnat "oreaking of the bread" (Luke 24:31, 35).

That moment of discovery probably was the most thrilling incident experienced by either of tnose Emmaus men

during their entire lifetimes. Now they were in the
presence of this illustrious guest.

Nevertheless, that exultant joy was destined to last
only a moment, for immediately ". . . he vanished out of
their sight" (Luke 24:31). How did Jesus "vanish" from the
presence of these two men? Did he simply evaporate in a
mysterious miraculous manner? Or, after handing them the
bits of bread, may it not be that he suddenly rose, turned
about, and went out the door? This latter supposition would
seem the more likely.

Presumably assuming that he had gone out for only a few
moments of privacy, the men probably occupied those seconds
by recounting how they were stirred by his conversations
with them along the way (Luke 24:32). "And they said, one
to the other, 'Were not our hearts burning within us while
he was speaking to us on the way, when he opened to us the
Scriptures?'" The two hosts must have assumed that Jesus
soon would return through that door, recline with them
again, and share the evening meal.

While breaking the bread, Jesus apparently changed his
mind with regard to going home. Instead, he decided that he
was not going to do the cowardly act of fleeing to Galilee.
No! He had suddenly resolved that he would return to
Jerusalem and face his persecutors and crucifiers there all
over again. Because of his sudden determination to get back

to Jerusalem at the earliest possible moment, he left his meal at Emmaus uneaten.

Minutes passed and Jesus did not return to the Emmaus meal. After a time the two hosts must have become alarmed and have gone out to search for him. Apparently they were unable to find a trace of his whereabouts. He evidently had gone from their home and had vanished into the darkness of night.

Where had he gone? To attempt a night search for him would have been fruitless. So they probably returned to their meal in consternation. After having graced their home with his presence, what a dissappointment that Jesus had so quickly departed from them!

After the two men recovered somewhat from their shock, they decided that they had better return to Jerusalem and report Jesus' movements to the disciples. "So they rose up that very hour and returned to Jerusalem" (Luke 24:33). As they apparently took slightly different paths, the Emmaus men did not intercept Jesus on the way. Although they started later, the two outwalked Jesus in his weakened condition and arrived in Jerusalem first.

Sixth Easter Report: From the Upper Room at Midnight

Mary Magdalene undoubtedly was responsible for luring the disaffected and frightened disciples from their places

of hiding for an Easter night gathering in the upper room of
her rented quarters. Mark's portraying the disciples in a
most unfavoraole light that evening may have been a
contributing reason why Mark's whole ending, as seen
earlier, was removed from that gospel. Only Luke has
salvaged from Mark's first unexpurgated edition a few verses
from that presumably valid account of what occurred on that
emotion-filled evening (Luke 24:33-49). Verse 33 lists the
assembled group as consisting of "the eleven . . . and those
who were with them." This latter phrase probably referred
to the women followers.

That company must have been taken by surprise when the
two men from Emmaus entered. The members of that inner
circle were startled when the Emmaus pair told how they had
encountered Jesus on the road in mid-afternoon, how he had
explained the Scriptures to them, how he ostensibly had
accepted the hospitality of their home for the evening meal
and night, "how he became recognized by them in the breaking
of the bread" (Luke 24:35), and then how he so suddenly
vanished from them.

Possibly before the Emmaus pair had completed their
story, that company became astounded as Jesus himself set
foot into their place of meeting and stood in their midst.
"As they were saying this, Jesus himself stood in the midst
of them and said to them, 'Peace to you.' But they were

startled and frightened, and supposed that they saw a spirit. And he said to them, 'Why are you troubled and why do questionings arise in your minds? See my hands and my feet, that it is I myself. Handle me and see, for a spirit does not have flesh and bones as you see that I have'" (Luke 24:36-40).

If one loves history rather than theological fiction, the foregoing words are some of the most distinctive in the New Testament. Luke, probably following the lost Marcan version, has relayed to us what is evidently the only true surviving picture of Easter evening. And what a picture it is! How different from what one would have expected! How different from what falsifiers of Easter have been telling us from that first Easter to the present! That the story is so radically different from what one would have expected is the most certain assurance that this is the true picture of the first-Easter evening.

One is struck at the outset by the inability of the disciples and associates to deal with this totally unexpected occurrence of finding Jesus alive on Easter night and in their midst. They were completely nonplussed as to how they might deal with this unbelievable event. It was clear to them that those moments on the cross had brought an end to his life and career.

Members of that upper-room company seem even to have
avoided Jesus' presence. One can see them drawing away in
fright and huddling in one corner of the room, with him in
the opposite one. There is no record that anyone dared to
touch him. He held out his hands and feet and invited the
disciples to feel his real physical presence, but no one
seemed to respond, preferring to keep distance from him as
they cowered in fear.

These reactions show that the upper-room gathering did
not believe that Jesus was a physical person. Since they
regarded him as only a spirit or disembodied ghost, they
avoided contact lest they become contaminated. As they
refused his invitation to touch his hands and feet, the
exposed parts of his body, the disciples presumably
continued in their illusion that they were seeing only an
apparition.

In a last attempt to dissuade the company of their
misconception, that he was but a spirit, Jesus resorted to
the final means of proof that he was not such. "And when
they still disbelieved (for joy) and wondered, he said to
them, 'Have you anything here to eat?' They gave a piece of
broiled fish, and he took it and ate before them" (Luke
24:41-43).

In light of the total account of that evening's
occurrences, it is evident that "for joy" in verse 41 is an

interpolation stuck in by some reader or editor to bring
that record into harmony with later suppositions concerning
that evening. The lack of joy in the upper room on that
occasion was quite evident. One would have expected that
the whole group would have burst forth into jubilation at
his entry. Instead, they were petrified and speechless.

Throughout antiquity and the Old Testament there was
the belief that supernatural beings do not partake of mortal
food. By eating that piece of broiled fish, presumably cold
and left over from the evening meal, Jesus was giving those
doubters the ultimate proof that his was a real earthy
physical body and not a disembodied ghost. However, there
is no reason to believe that the disciples, and others
present, were convinced by even this final demonstration.

Jesus had two times of supreme disappointment during
so-called Holy Week. The first occurred as he was about to
take his last breath on the cross and saw that he was being
forsaken by everyone. His followers, including the
disciples, had deserted him and were allowing him to die a
friendless person. But Jesus' most bitter anguish was
expressed in his final moments as he poured fourth his grief
over the way even God had deserted him and allowed him to be
the victim of such a terrible death (Mark 15:34; Matthew
27:46): "My God, my God, why have (even) you forsaken me?"

The other pathos-filled experience consisted in the alienation with which he was confronted on Easter night as his disciples virtually rejected him. Jesus apparently was unable to cope with such extreme estrangement as was present on Easter evening.

At that point, evidently in a desperate attempt to salvage the situation, Jesus gave a short speech to the assembled group, whether or not they wanted to listen (Luke 24:44-49). In Part III it will be shown that Luke likely has made certain expansions in transcribing that final address. Attention here will be devoted to the presumably authentically reported elements in that terminal discourse. It consisted of two parts, three verses in each.

First was Jesus' explanation why his meeting death in Jerusalem was not wholly unexpected. He virtually repeated what he had said to the two men on the Emmaus road, citing "'things . . . which are written in the law of Moses, and the prophets, and the psalms concerning me.' Then he opened their minds that they might understand the Scriptures" (Luke 24:44-46).

Preceding section 4 dealt at length with what passages Jesus may have used in opening up the Scriptures concerning his fate in Jerusalem, and what he might have said. Jesus undoubtedly pointed out that although Israel was privileged to have a superb line of prophets, this was the country that

killed its prophets. On Palm Sunday Jesus had gone into
Jerusalem "weeping" because that city was famed for killing
the prophets who came to her (Luke 19:41-44). Jesus
considered himself in the prophetic succession and this
portended ill for him as he dared to enter that bastion of
reactionary religion.

The other half of Jesus' valedictory address, according
the Luke 24:47-49, consisted in calling his disciples to
action. From their evident attitude he must have discerned
that they were regarding nis work as having ended in a
fizzle. He now indicated that he was relying on them to
continue it.

Mark 1:15 records that Jesus began his ministry by
calling upon people to "repent and believe in the gospel."
In what proved to be his final words to the eleven Jesus
commissioned them to go forth with the same purpose and
preach repentance in his name. According to the usual
rendition, this call to repentance was to be extended "to
all tne nations, beginning from Jerusalem" (Luke 24:47).

It is to be doubted that Jesus committed his disciples
to a world-wide mission "to all the nations" as verse 47 is
probably inadvisedly translated. Jesus was a small-town man
whose perspective did not extend much beyond the borders of
Palestine. He never went far from his home base, and did
most of his teaching in tne three small towns of Capernaum,
Chorazin, and Bethsaida (Luke 10:13-15; Matthew 11:21-23).

The Aramaic word underlying the strategic term in Luke 24:47 has consonants a-r-ts and may be translated earth or land. Here, as most other occurrences in the Bible, translators have taken the wrong alternative by translating earth or world. That the gospel should be preached "to all nations" is therefore probably not the proper rendition. The alternative "land" (of Palestine) would seem more likely.

The Greek author of Luke 24:47 has probably sensed Jesus' meaning most accurately by using the Greek word ethnoi. In other words, this key word had ethnic rather than nationalistic significance. Jesus was urging that the disciples should preach to all "ethnic groups" in the entire land of Palestine: Samaritans, Syrians, Lebanese, and all other foreigners sojourning in that land, as well as to Jews.

The Synoptic Gospels indicate that Jesus' ministry, from baptism to crucifixion, had lasted only a year. As part of even that year was lost to actual teaching by the forty days in the wilderness and several retreats outside Galilee, his public work had lasted perhaps only about nine months and it had touched only a small portion of Palestine. Now ne was calling upon the disciples to extend his ministry to the entire land of Palestine, including Judea.

However, Jesus felt the need to caution his disciples against approaching this evangelistic effort precipitously or halfheartedly. He therefore advised that they should remain in Jerusalem until such time as they might regain the measure of God's spirit and its accompanying power which they had displayed during the classic days of his ministry (Luke 24:49).

With that admonition, according to Luke's gospel, that historic evening came to an end. There is no indication whether Jesus was able, through his remarks, to break the estrangement barrier. There also is no evidence that any of the assembled group spoke even a single word to him during the entire evening.

It might be guessed that Jesus' words fell on deaf ears, that the potentially historic meeting on that first-Easter night ended in an impasse, and that Jesus left discouraged. Instead of being a night of triumph, it appears to have ended in mutual despair.

At that point the valid Easter story came to an end, without telling how Jesus made his exit from the group. He probably withdrew, in extreme disappointment, into the darkness. This was the end of the first Easter, as it really occurred.

Curtain Call on the First Easter

Now that this survey of the valid account regarding occurrences on the First Easter has been completed, it is a fitting time to look back and see that day in perspective.

The results of this search must be pitted against the usual supposition that the first Easter was a day of multiplied cosmic miracles, with great rejoicing and excitement in Jerusalem. It is portrayed as the greatest day in the history of the Christian Church, with the populace of that city in exultation over what had occurred during those momentous hours.

The combined Marcan and Lucan authentic witness indicates the exact opposite. Because of the virtual news blackout over the Passover celebration from Friday evening to Saturday evening, most residents of the supposed "Holy City" presumably did not hear about Jesus having been crucified until Sunday, following Passover. The populace was depressed because their new "king," who they hoped would bring liberation from Roman rule, had been killed.

Even as late as Easter evening only the inner circle of Jesus' followers seem to have known of what had transpired at the tomb on Easter morning. They were so frightened and stunned by what had occurred that they were saying little or nothing about it to people outside their inner circle. This reticence may have been partly from fear of being arrested by the authorities as accomplices of Jesus.

There was no semblance of rejoicing among the disciples, but only consternation, bewilderment, and disbelief over what they had heard and seen. Their

Messianic dream had collapsed, their movement was at an end, and now, menaced by Jesus' continuing ghost, Easter had landed his followers in deep despair.

The surprise and incredulity of the disciples and women on Easter morning and forenoon with regard to Jesus being alive again adds up to the assurance that he never gave any prediction about being resurrected from the dead. He evidently had warned the disciples on various occasions that persisting in their ministry, especially if it were to be extended to Jerusalem, would likely mean dissension, opposition, persecution, and even possible death (Mark 13:9; 10:35-45; Luke 10:3; 21:12; 12:51-52; Matthew 10:16-18, 34-36; 20:20-28).

However, similar passages in Mark 8:31; 9:31; 10:33-34 and parallels in the other gospels make Jesus to predict his death by crucifixion in Jerusalem, followed by resurrection on the third day. In these instances Jesus' general predictions were evidently "brought up to date" by some later interpolator and made specific to fit the events as they transpired on Easter weekend. Such enhancements placed on the lips of Jesus are similar to the "prophecies post eventum," (after the event) that later writers inserted in the Old Testament to magnify an earlier prophet's predictive ability. That there was no thought of a resurrection in the minds of either Jesus or the disciples as they approached

Holy Week accounts for their being so completely unprepared
for what occurred on Easter day.

The Church stands indebted especially to Mark for
having given to us his eight-verse presumably valid report
of Easter dawn at the tomb. Credit also goes to Luke for
having salvaged the facts in Mark's lost ending concerning
the situation in Jerusalem at midforenoon, afternoon,
evening, and night of that notable day. Disappointingly
meager though these facts are for reconstructing the history
of such a significant day, that this much authentic material
has survived should be regarded by the Christian Church as a
precious treasure.

Seventh Easter Report: The Lost Monday Morning Dispatch

By contrast with the foregoing series of valid reports
that came from Jerusalem on Easter day, at intervals from
dawn to midnight, there also must have been in this
succession a terminal dispatch that probably was issued on
Monday forenoon. That news item unfortunately has been
lost. Only through inferences can one speculate as to its
contents.

After the excitement of Easter day and night, Jesus'
subsequent acts, if there had been any, certainly would have
been recorded with the utmost detail. The absence of any

such post-Easter authentic records indicates that the last time anyone saw Jesus alive was on Easter night in the upper room.

How did it happen that Jesus dropped from sight so suddenly? Mark's original ending, later expurgated from that gospel, may have told tne real story. That loss is irreparable when it comes to recording the last moments of Jesus' life.

Regarding Jesus' disappearance two avenues of speculation seem possible. According to the first, Jesus may have disappeared from the upper room as he disappeared from the home in Emmaus, none of the hosts having been aware in either case that he was leaving until too late to intercept him. The rather insuperable difficulty with this supposition is that it is hard to believe that he would not have been recognized by anyone during subsequent days.

Since the authentic record in Luke stops suddenly at approximately midnight on Easter day, this indicates that Jesus probably died of heart failure shortly thereafter or on the following morning. His death would have come about in consequence of the prolonged chain of accumulated strains and anxieties endured in the course of his arrest and trials, the ordeal of torture on the cross, the agonies of finding himself alive but helplessly bound in an isolated tomp, the exertions and exciting events of Easter day,

together with walking to Emmaus and returning presumably
with no nourishment since Thursday evening except for a
broiled leftover fish on Easter night.

As Moses died in the hour of his achievement, when he
gained his first view of the Promised Land, so Jesus may
have been overpowered by death at the moment of his triumph
over the Thursday-Sunday events as he finally found himself
somewhat relaxed after that long tensity.

Comparable deaths take place today at similar moments
of triumph and accomplishment. Such have been experienced
by two of this author's personal acquaintances. President
William Wickenden of Case Institute of Technology at
Cleveland, Ohio, looked forward avidly to his retirement.
It became official at 12 o'clock midnight on August 31,
1947. Although apparently in good health, he died suddenly
of heart failure two hours later at 2:00 a.m., on the portal
of his eagerly anticipated retirement. Like Moses, he too
died the moment his work of the years was completed.

Doctor Donald Evans, State Superintendant of the
Universalist churches in Ohio, was much interested in
promoting a proposed merger with the Unitarian denomina-
tion. At the state meeting in Akron, Ohio, on June 21,
1963, as the final vote was being taken, he was sitting at
his official desk. When it was announced that the vote was
favorable, he instantly collapsed before the whole assembly,

slumped over, and was dead. The joy of that moment of
achievement was too much for him to bear.

In harmony with the Moses-Wickended-Evans pattern,
Jesus may have died suddenly from heart failure on Monday
morning during the anticlimatic calm and letdown that often
sets in following achievement of great triumph. In that
event Jesus likely would have been entombed in some more
insignificant place than Joseph of Arimathea's presumably
luxurious sepulchre which he had occupied before. This time
Jesus apparently did not revive, as after his Friday
entombment.

The body, and later the bones, of Jesus may well have
been disposed of according to the usual burial practices in
Jerusalem at that time. As burial in rock tombs or
sepulchres was costly and space was limited, such disposals
usually were regarded as only temporary. Skeletons were
removed after a year or two, when all flesh had become
decomposed. The bones then were detached from each other
and packed into bone boxes called ossuaries, approximately
twenty-four inches long by eighteen inches wide by eighteen
inches high. To save space these ossuaries were placed on
top of each other from floor to ceiling in buildings called
charnel houses.

Pursuant to this custom, the bones of Jesus may
actually survive today among the collection of ossuaries

from that period in Jerusalem. G. Ernest Wright describes
this possibility: "It was Jewish practice, when the bodies
of the deceased had decomposed and room was needed for new
burials, to collect the bones and place them in small stone
boxes, now called ossuaries . . . A great many of these
ossuaries have been found, dating from the 1st centuries
B.C. and A.D., and the names of the dead were frequently
carved on them . . . There is even a 'Jeshua (Jesus) son of
Joseph.'"[2]

This name, which appears in the New Testament Greek as
Jesus and in the Hebrew Scriptures as Joshua, had been
carried by only one prominent person in pre-Christian
biblical history, Joshua the successor to Moses. Throughout
the Old Testament the name appears, on an average, only once
every two centuries. Only a single occurrence is found in
the vast intertestament literature, Joshua (Jesus) ben
Sirach. The rarity of this name is indicated further by the
fact that it never is found in the New Testament except as
carried by Jesus of Nazareth.

Since that name was so uncommon, it would appear
possible that the bones of this Jesus may actually be those
of Jesus of Nazareth. The additional mention that Joseph
was his father would seem to bend the possibility into a
strong probability. It therefore may well be that the bones
in the ossuary in question are those of Jesus and that they

bear witness to his death in Jerusalem. As to how people in the Early Church were to deal with this presumed predicament of apparently having in their midst Jesus' corpse, and then his bones, more will be said in Part III.

The ultimate death of Jesus was probably the main reason that Easter day made so little impact upon Jerusalem, as well as upon Jesus' actual and potential followers. This all adds up to why the Church was not born on Easter day but seven weeks later at Pentecost when the occupants of the upper room believed that the Holy Spirit descended upon them and for the first time the movement got really on the way.

There will continue the regret that the seventh dispatch from Jerusalem, concerning what finally happened to Jesus, has been lost. The original ending to Mark's gospel probably described the death and final burial. But that account presumably proved to be such an embarrassment to the Early Church that the entire genuine conclusion to that gospel was removed and unfortunately has perished. Even so, the faint hope will persist that a manuscript with the original ending intact may yet be found in some archaeological excavation.

Notes   Part I

1.   James Hastings, <u>Dictionary of the Bible</u>, New York,
      Charles Scribner's Sons, Vol. III, 1900, p. 253.

2.   G. Ernest Wright, <u>Biblical Archaeology</u>, Philadelphia,
      Westminster Press, 1957, p. 242.

PART II

WAYS OF ACCOUNTING FOR JESUS' EASTER APPEARANCES

Resurrection or Immortality?

Learning the authentic facts, from Mark and Luke in Part I, regarding what occurred on the first Easter was rather easy. However, to explain what took place is far more difficult. From New Testament days to the present, interpreters have been confronted with the puzzling problem of how to explain Jesus' appearances on Easter day.

Although, according to the usual superficial assumption there is only one answer to this problem, careful studies show that no less than seven divergent interpretations are actively advanced or reflected within the New Testament itself.

This quest runs into the almost universal confusing of the terms resurrection and immortality, using them interchangeably. The intellectual fog caused by failing to make the proper distinction between these two fundamentally different types of life survival must be cleared away before one can appraise accurately the Easter appearances of Jesus.

According to resurrection belief, the body is a unit being. At death the whole person does and becomes subject to decay and ultimate extinction. By resurrection, whether sooner or at the end of time, the body is completely reintegrated as an intelligent being, exactly as it was formerly during life. In the case of resurrection one should not speak of a soul. The person, both now and in the resurrection, is only an animated body.

By contrast, according to the immortality concept we are dual beings made up of body and soul. At death, only the physical body dies. It is thought to moulder away and is never reintegrated again. Conversely, the soul never dies. At death it simply leaves the body, supposedly to continue its existence in more ethereal regions for an endless eternity. As resurrection is oriented toward the physical, immortality is weighted on the side of the nonphysical.

Bearing in mind the difference between these two fundamentally different types of life survival, we proceed to pass in review the various New Testament explanations of Jesus' appearances on that first Easter.

I. Physical Death and Bodily Resurrection

First to be mentioned is the explanation of Easter that has become normative in the Church through the centuries. This is the belief that Jesus died on the cross on Good Friday afternoon and then, after having been dead for parts of three days, suddenly came back to life miraculously on the following Sunday morning. This event is commonly referred to as his resurrection from the dead or the bodily resurrection of Jesus.

To those who conceive the main purpose of religion as
getting its adherents to Heaven, belief in the bodily
resurrection of Christ is virtually the whole of
Christianity. His resurrection therefore has come to be
thought of as the keystone doctrine that holds the arch of
Christian faith together. If a keystone is removed, the
whole arch crashes into a pile of rubble. In the same way
it is generally believed that if the doctrine of the bodily
resurrection were removed, the whole of Christianity would
collapse. This makes the dogma of Jesus' physical
resurrection of the utmost importance for orthodox
Christianity.

Christians of conservative bent have devised what seems
to them a foolproof set of inquiries which they put in rapid
succession to those who are being interrogated with regard
to their religion. After being asked whether they believe
in the verbal inspiration and inerrancy of the Bible, the
virgin birth, that Jonah lived in the big fish's belly three
days and was vomited out alive, the ultimate confrontation
usually is, "Do you believe that Jesus was resurrected
physically from the dead after three days?"

The answer to this final question is supposed to be the
ultimate faithometer reading which tells infallibly whether
or not the questioned person is "a Christian." In case of a
negative answer, it is assumed by the interrogator that the

one making reply has no valid religion. If the answer is in the affirmative, the individual's Christianity is assumed to be acceptable.

It will be surprising to see, in subsequent pages, how little New Testament support there is for this doctrine. It is even possible that no one held this view on that first Easter day in Jerusalem except the centurian guard at the tomb area. This is a classic example of an extreme minority New Testament item of faith becoming the normative belief of the Church.

II. Immortalized and Glorified from the Cross

In light of Paul's frequent reference to "the resurrection," New Testament interpreters almost unanimously have assumed that the apostle to the Gentiles was an adherent of the position just described. However, closer examination of Acts and his writings reveal that he held a diametrically opposite position.

Since Paul was more in harmony with the views of Jesus on this matter, the Master himself should be consulted. His statement to the thief on the cross indicates that Jesus believed in immortality rather than resurrection. He said, "Today you shall be with me in Paradise," not "Three days from now when I am resurrected you shall be with me in Paradise" (Luke 23:43). Jesus apparently assumed that both the thief and himself would be ushered into Paradise at the moments of their repective bodily deaths.

The same belief in ongoing immortal life was expressed in what according to Luke was Jesus' last statement from the cross: "Father, into your hands I commend my spirit" (Luke 23:46). This identical view was attributed to Jesus in the Fourth Gospel in the statement "whoever lives, and believes in me, shall never die" (John 11:26). He did not say, "whoever believes in me shall be resurrected at the end of time."

Evidently Paul held the immortality concept with respect to Jesus. Two items in his point of view show that Paul did not believe in the bodily resurrection of Jesus. The apostle's key statement on this matter is, "Flesh and blood cannot inherit the kingdom of God, nor does corruption inherit incorruption" (I Corinthians 15:50).

Another fundamental evidence for Paul's not believing that Jesus was physically resurrected on Easter day lies in his assertion that what he calls the resurrection body is quite different from the mortal physical body. His classic presentation on this theme in I Corinthians 15:35-58 snows that in life survival, the physical body is replaced by a "spirit body" (vs. 44).

In light of these statements in I Corinthians, Paul was certain that reports of Jesus having been dead for parts of

three days and then resurrected as a physical body on Easter
morning were not true.

Nevertheless, strange as it may seem, the "resurrection
of Christ" is basic in Paul's theology. If what this
apostle calls the resurrection did not take place on Easter
day, when then did it occur? Because Paul places his great
stress on the cross and the crucifixion, it becomes apparent
that what he calls the "resurrection" took place on the
cross rather than in an Easter-morning tomb. In other
words, Paul has confused his terms by speaking of what he
assumed happened on the cross as resurrection ratner than
immortality.

Since Paul was convinced by experience that Jesus nad
become the triumphant Christ, the apostle was forced to
conclude that there had been no interruption in Jesus' life
and that he never died, except physically. His soul lived
on and, in the final moment on Calvary's cross when Jesus
breathed his last mortal breath, was immortalized and
miraculously transformed on that Friday afternoon into a
supernatural being with a spirit body.

Because of nis obedience to sacrificial death on the
cross, that act purchased salvation for all believing
mankind. As a reward, Christ was at that moment glorified
to become the Lord of ages. This was the immortal Christ
who struck Paul down on the Damascus road and became the

major inspiration and guide of his life.

Since Paul derived his whole theology from what he
assumed to have happened on the cross, rather than on Easter
day, he was almost vehement in insisting that the whole
validity of Christ rested on this belief in his
"resurrection." Paul even went so far as to say that if
what he called the "resurrection" did not occur, nothing
would be left of our religion, it might as well be
forgotten, and "we would be of all men most pitiable" (I
Corinthians 15:19).

As Paul did nis writing before any gospel, with a
record of Easter events, was produced, it might be contended
that he knew nothing of any Easter day or special
occurrences thereon. However, since he was in Jerusalem so
shortly after the event, at the stoning of Stephen, and
since Paul became the leading persecutor of the Church, he
must have known what reportedly had occurred on Easter day.

Paul apparently did not give credence to any events
which supposedly had taken place on that day. When he made
his first postconversion visit to Jerusalem, and spent
fifteen days with Peter and James (Galatians 1:18-20), they
probably tried to recount to him the Easter highlights.
However, Paul's letters indicate that he would not listen.
He was so certain that the whole divine drama of salvation
and Christ's glorification had been enacted from the cross

that he presumably refused to hear anything Peter and James
tried to tell him about the life, teachings, and religion of
Jesus, as well as the events of Easter day (Galatians
1:18-19).

The ultimate word regarding Paul and that notable day
is that Easter was completely ignored by him and his
followers. In all his letters Paul made no mention of any
events on that day, or even that there ever was such a day.
To him Easter not only had no significance but also was a
day of physical emphases which distracted attention from
what he considered the real day of Christian origins, the
greatest day in history, the day of Jesus' immortalizing on
Calvary. How could Jesus have been resurrected on Easter
day when he had achieved the immortal state three days
previously on the cross? Consequently, to Paul and
subsequent writers of epistles, Easter was treated as an
unmentionable big zero.

Because Paul regarded crucifixion Friday as the
greatest day in world history, under his influence it came
to be called "Good Friday." Similarly, the Friday cross
became the symbol of Christianity rather than any Easter-day
imagery connected with an empty tomb.

III.   Jesus Never Died but Invaded and Conquered Hell

Even within the New Testament there are various shades
of immortality belief with regard to Jesus on Good
Friday-Easter. While the previous view conceived that Jesus
left his wracked body on the cross and entered the overworld
to receive the reward promised by his Father, a variant view
conceived of him also not dying on the cross but leaving his
body for a three-day stint of service in the underworld.

This view follows along the line of ancient Egyptian
concepts of life survival. Those people were among the
first to develop the belief that such a procedure is
possible. They were certain that the individual is a
duality of body and soul, with only the body dying at the
moment called death. Freed from its physical encumbrance,
the soul or Ka continued to live on, liberated to roam
wherever it might wish. Independent of space, it could
travel throughout the universe. The meticulous care exerted
in the embalming rites was in order to retain the physical
organism intact so the Ka could return at any time it might
choose. Magnificent tombs were constructed at great expense
and effort to enshrine the treasured body so the Ka might
enjoy seasons of homeness throughout eternity.

Popular Tibetan thought advances one stage beyond the
Egyptian by insisting that even in ordinary life the soul

can leave its body, roam about, return, and completely
reanimate its inert physical form at will. The following
story offers an excellent present-day illustration of this
belief.

In a certain village, a man-eating tiger had menaced
the inhabitants for weeks, always coming down a certain path
to seize and devour people of that settlement. Finally one
of the citizens volunteered to put a stop to this carnage.
He went up the path down which the tiger was accustomed to
come. At the edge of the village he lay across the trail
and disembodied himself. Then, unencumbered by his fleshly
form, in his soul state he went traveling all over the
earth. Since wild animals, according to Tibetian assertion,
are afraid of a desouled body, the tiger caused the people
of the village no more harm.

After some months of free roaming, the man returned.
He found that while away a bird had built a nest in his hair
and had presumably raised a brood of young. Entering
soulwise into his body again, he got up, went to his home,
and proceeded to resume his life in its normal way. By
disembodying himself, and then eventually returning to pick
up his physical form, he had gotten a wonderful vacation and
at the same time had saved his village from harm.

It was no strain on the imagination for certain people
in the Early Church to believe that Jesus had done virtually
the same. According to this out-of-body view, held by some
late New Testament and apocryphal gospel-writers, Jesus did
not die on the cross but abandoned his body and left the
cross at approximately 3 p.m. on Good Friday afternoon for
necessary service in the nether world. At that moment he
descended into Hell where he spent the remaining hours of
Friday, all of Saturday, and the nighttime hours of Sunday.
In those regions of fiery torture he conquered the
fortresses of the underworld and put an end to Satan's
unrestrained despotic reign. All this was summed up in
Jesus' breaking the power of death which had prevailed over
the human race from some four millennia, since the Eve-Adam
disobedience in Eden.

With that herculean task accomplished, Christ returned
from the underworld, victorious over death. This was the
greatest gift the world has known, the gift of eternal
salvation for all believing human beings. Upon returning to
Jerusalem in the hours of darkness on Sunday morning he
found that his body had been removed from the cross and had
been placed in the tomb of Joseph of Arimathea. Christ
rolled away the stone from the tomb door, removed the
graveclothes bindings from his body, entered it again, rose,
left the tomb, and met the Easter early-morning visitants.

New Testament expression of the belief that Jesus spent the interval between Friday afternoon and Sunday morning in the conquest of Hell, also conducting evangelistic services there, is found in I Peter 3:19-20. There it is told how ". . . he went and preached to the spirits in prison, who aforetime were disobedient . . ."

Even the Apostles' Creed is inconsistent with itself by reason of holding variant positions at this point. The view of Easter described first in this chapter is expressed in the creed by the words, "Was crucified, dead, and buried: . . The third day he rose again from the dead." Into the midst of this, in wholly inconsistent manner, has been placed the statement, "He descended into Hell." Removal of this clause from some current printings does not nullify the fact that it was present in all early copies. That this belief regarding Jesus' activity in Hell between Good Friday and Easter should have wedged its way even into the Apostles' Creed is significant.

The classic account of how Jesus conducted his campaign against Hell is found in Part II of the Acts of Pilate, the portion called "The Descent into Hell."[1] That document tells how Jesus went directly from the cross to invade Hell. The following descriptions and quotations are from the Latin B. manuscript.

As it became apparent that something spectacular was about to transpire, the inhabitants of Hell are recorded to have said, "When therefore we were holden in hell in darkness and the shadow of death, suddenly there shone upon us a great light, and hell did tremble, and the gates of death. And there was heard the voice of the Son of the most high Father, as it were tne voice of a great thundering, and it proclaimed aloud and began: Draw back, O princes, your gates, remove your everlasting doors: Christ the Lord the king of glory approacheth to enter in."[2]

The consternation of Satan and his official entourage is then described. "Then came Satan the prince of death, fleeing in fear and saying to his ministers and unto the hells: O my ministers and all the hells, come together, and shut your gates, set in place the bars of iron, and fight boldly and withstand, that we that hold them be not made captive in bonds. Then were all his evil ministers troubled, and began to shut the gates of death with all diligence, and by little to make fast the locks and the bars of iron, and to take fast in hand all their instruments, and to utter howlings with dreadful and hideous voice."[3]

Following a frantic conversation between Satan and Hell, Adam finally joined the interchange. "But our holy father Adam made answer unto Satan thus: O prince of death, wherefore fearest thou and tremblest? Behold the Lord

cometh which shall destroy all thy creatures, and thou shalt
be taken captive of him and be bound, world without
end."[4] That is, all Satan's subsidiary staff of helpers
were to be destroyed.

Thereupon David joined in, saying, "Let them give
thanks unto the Lord, even his mercies: and his wonders
unto the children of men. For he hath broken the gates of
brass and smitten the bars of iron in sunder."[5]

At that point all "the holy patriarchs and prophets"
began to recognize each other and unite in a song of
triumph. "Then all the saints rejoicing in the light of the
Lord and at the sight of their father Adam, and at the
answer of all the patriarchs and prophets, cried out,
saying: Allelulia, blessed is he that cometh in the name of
the Lord. So that at the cry of them Satan feared, and
sought a way to flee by, and could not, . . ."[6]

"And again there came the voice of the Son of the most
high Father, as the voice of a great thunder, saying: Lift
up, O princes, your gates, and be ye lift up, ye everlasting
doors, and the King of glory shall come in. Then Satan and
Hell cried out, saying: Who is this King of glory? And it
was answered them by the Lord's voice: The Lord strong and
mighty, the Lord mighty in battle . . . Then the holy
David's anger was kindled against Satan, and he cried
aloud: Open, thou most foul one, thy gates, that the King

of glory may come in. Likewise also the saints of God rose
up against Satan and would have laid hold on him and parted
him among them."[7]

At this point the action began to take place. "And lo,
suddenly Hell did quake, and the gates of death and the
locks were broken small, and the bars of iron broken, and
fell to the ground, and all things were laid open. And
Satan remained in the midst and stood put to confusion and
cast down, and bound with a fetter about his feet. And
behold, the Lord Jesus Christ coming in the glory of the
light of the height, in meekness, great and yet humble,
bearing a chain in his hands bound therewith the neck of
Satan, and also, binding his hands behind his back, cast him
backward into Tartarus, and set his holy foot upon his
throat and said: Throughout all ages hast thou done much
evil and hast never been quiet at any time. To-day do I
deliver thee unto eternal fire. And he called Hell quickly
and gave him commandment, saying: Take this most evil and
wicked one and hold him in thy keeping until that day when I
shall command thee. And he took him from beneath the Lord's
feet, and he was cast down together with him into the depth
of the bottomless pit."[8]

"Then the Lord Jesus, the Savior of all men, pitiful
and most gracious, greeted Adam with kindness, saying unto
him: Peace be unto thee, Adam, and unto thy children unto

everlasting ages. Amen. Then Father Adam cast himself at
the Lord's feet, and rose up and kissed his hands, and shed
abundant tears, saying: Behold the hands which formed me:
testifying unto all. And he said to the Lord: Thou art
come, O King of glory, to set men free and gather them to
thine everlasting kingdom. Then our mother Eve also in like
manner cast herself at the feet of the Lord, and rose up and
kissed his hands, and shed tears abundantly, and said:
Behold the hands which fashioned me: testifying unto
all."[9]

"Then all the saints adoring him cried out, saying:
Blessed is he that cometh in the name of the Lord: God the
Lord hath showed us light. Amen throughout all ages.
Alleluia, world without end: laud, honour, might, and
glory, because thou hast come from on high to visit us. And
they gathered them beneath the hands of the Lord, singing
always Alleluia, and rejoicing together at the glory. Then
the Savior searched throughout and did bite hell (al. hell
was in affliction), forasmuch as he cast down part into
Tartarus, and part he brought again with him on high."[10]

"Then all the saints of God besought the Lord that he
would leave the sign of victory -- even of the holy cross --
in hell, that the wicked ministers thereof might not prevail
to keep back any that was accused, whom the Lord absolved.
And so it was done, and the Lord set his cross in the midst

of hell, which is the sign of victory; and it shall remain there for ever."[11]

"These be the testimonies, beloved brethren, of Karinus and Leucius, concerning Christ the Son of God and his holy acts in Hell: unto whom let us all give praise and glory unto ages without end. Amen."[12]

Another rather extensive account of Jesus' descent into Hell is found in Part I of the Gospel of Bartholomew[13] but we shall refrain from quoting any of that here. The Book of the Resurrection of Christ by Bartholomew the Apostle[14] also has some writing on this subject, telling how "He wrought havoc in Hell, breaking the doors, binding the demons Beliar and Melkir . . . and delivered Adam and the holy souls . . . only three souls were left in it (those of Herod, Cain, and Judas, . . .)."[15]

According to this view, the phenomenon of Easter consisted merely in Jesus' return to earth from his victorious conquest of Hell. On that Sunday morning at approximately 6:00 a.m. he returned to Jerusalem to the sepulchre and picked up his body again. Or, perhaps it would be better to say he reincarnated himself in it. In this way a significant segment of the Early Church accounted for how it came about that Jesus was physically alive in Jerusalem on Easter day.

The term resurrection should properly not be connected with such an explanation for, according to it, Jesus, the author of immortality, never died. Contrary to the unity of being that is assumed in the resurrection theory, the foregoing descent-into-Hell assumption operates on the belief that a sharp dualism and relative independence exist within the individual between body and soul.

Since according to this explanation Jesus did not die on the cross, salvation could not have been gained through the death of Jesus. Rather, along the lines of this belief, salvation was achieved through Jesus' victorious battling of Hell during those parts of three days that he spent there subjugating it.

IV.   Metaphysical Ghost Appearances or Apparitions

The opinion clearly indicated by the disciples in the upper room was that Jesus had not experienced a physical resurrection on Easter day. Rather, what the disciples saw on that evening was thought by them to be but a spiritual manifestation or apparition. Therefore, "they were terrified and frightened, and supposed that they beheld a spirit" (Luke 24:37). They cowered in fear before the eeriness of this supposed mystical appearance before them. To allay this illusion Jesus said to them, (Luke 24:38) "Why are you troubled? And why do questionings arise in your minds?"

Jesus tried two different methods to convince the disciples that he was not an apparition but the same physical presence they had gone about with during all the days of his ministry. He did this in the first instance by showing them his hands and his feet, the exposed parts of his body, where they could easily see and feel his flesh and bones. As he did so, he said, "See my hands and my feet, that it is I myself. Handle me, and see, for a spirit does not have flesh and bones as you behold me having. And when he had said this, he showed them his hands and his feet" (Luke 24:39-40).

The account does not go on to relate whether the disciples complied with Jesus' request. It may be guessed that they were so frightened, still thinking he was but a ghost, that none of them dared to touch him. This conclusion seems borne out by the statement which tells how "they still disbelieved" (Luke 24:41). That they disbelieved "for joy" can hardly be true since fright was the emotion of the moment, and they gave no evidence of being joyful. Those two words would seem to be a spurious interpolation.

Since Jesus' first method of convincing the disciples concerning his physical reality apparently had failed, he

tried another approach. "And while they still disbelieved
. . . and wondered, he said to them, 'Have you anything here
to eat?' And they gave him a piece of a broiled fish. And
he took it and ate before them" (Luke 24:41-43).

According to the beliefs in the biblical world, spirits
and ghosts never partake of mortal food. By eating that
broiled fish, Jesus was providing to the group that he was
not an apparition but a real physical presence. Whether the
disciples were finally convinced by this eating
demonstration is not stated. One may guess that they
persisted in believing that this was not the physical Jesus,
who had been placed in he tomb, but instead was an
incorporeal ghost and that the eating, in itself, was but a
further extension of the apparition.

Luke may have felt that even the afternoon and early
evening appearances of Jesus on the Emmaus road had been of
the same nature. This belief is implied in the suddenness
with which "Jesus himself drew near and went with them"
(Luke 24:15), that they did not recognize him (vs. 16), and
by the way he is described as presumably having instantly
"vanished out of their sight" (vs. 31). In fact, the two
Emmaus men may well have construed that the reason for not
eating with them was his being a ghostly apparition rather
than a real physical presence.

Since Luke's record of the Easter morning report has been basically copied from Mark's gospel, it seems to indicate that Jesus left the tomb as a physical person. However, in the Emmaus-road experiences and the midnight appearance in the upper room, Luke presumably gave his own interpretation of those events, which was that they were not physical but some sort of mystical manifestations.

This view is also expressed prominently in the Gospel of John. Because this apparition or spiritual appearance of Jesus was construed as so different from his physical presence, Mary Magdalene is represented as not realizing it was Jesus when she met him in the garden on Easter morning. The text says "she turned herself back and beheld Jesus standing, but she did not recognize that it was Jesus" (John 20:14).

That gospel further stresses this view by asserting that, on Easter evening, Jesus suddenly appeared before the disciples in the upper room even though the doors were closed. "When therefore it was evening on that day, the first of the week, and when for fear of the Jews the doors were shut where the disciples were, Jesus came and stood in the midst and said unto them, 'Peace to you'" (John 20:19).

The same ability of the spiritual or apparition Jesus to go through walls or doors is asserted again in describing his appearance to the disciples one week later, also in the upper room. "And after eight days his disciples again were within, and Thomas with them. Jesus came, the doors being shut, and stood in the midst and said, 'Peace to you'" (John 20:26).

The fact that Jesus apparently had not been seen during the intervening week fits with this view that his appearances on Easter and one week later were sporadic and mystical.

Although it is not specifically stated, the same view may be implied in John's recording of Jesus' last contact with the disciples. This differs from both the other three gospels and Acts in describing a third and final appearance of Jesus to the disciples on the shores of the Tiberian Sea, i.e., the Sea of Galilee. "After these things Jesus revealed himself again to the disciples at the Sea of Tiberias . . . This was now the third time that Jesus was revealed to the disciples after he was risen from the dead" (John 21:1, 14).

That Jesus is not represented as appearing in the form of his physical presence seems indicated by the statement that "the disciples did not recognize that it was Jesus" (vs. 4). This reason for nonrecognition is borne out by the verb which may be translated best by "revealed" or "manifested." The disciples apparently did not recognize him until he had wrought for them the miraculous draught of fishes and had prepared for them a meal of broiled fish on shore (vss. 6-11). That they are represented as continuing estranged and afraid to speak to him, is indicated by the statement: "And none of the disciples dared inquire of him, 'Who are you?' knowing that it was the Lord" (vs. 12). This last clause is clearly a later interpolation by an individual who wanted to save the recognition ability of the disciples.

In light of all these Johannine obervations, it is clear that the two Easter chapters in the Fourth Gospel mean to represent Jesus as not having appeared to the disciples in his physical likeness but in some different and awesome metaphysical form.

In the Church's earliest history the author of Acts 1:2-3 states that "the apostles" were favored by such occasional presumably mystical appearances during the "forty days" after Easter "by many proofs." This was in a sense but an extension of the belief, held in orthodox Jewish circles, that the spirit or soul of the deceased hovers around the home for some days before taking its final departure.

Paul also believed that all appearances reported after Calvary were nonphysical in nature. His listing of Jesus' manifestations tells how "he appeared to Cephas, then to the twelve, then he appeared to more than five hundred brethren

at once -- of whom the greater part remain until now
(although some have fallen asleep), then he appeared to
James, then to all the apostles, and last of all, as to the
untimely born, he appeared to me also" (I Corinthians
15:5-8).

The fact that neither the author of Acts nor Paul list
any transit of Jesus' physical presence from one geograph-
ical area to the next indicates that these appearances were
not to be thought of as physical. Instead, those sporadic
manifestations on Easter day and for some weeks thereafter
were construed as his metaphysical being, ghost, apparition,
or spirit body as Paul called it (I Corinthians 15:44-52).

It is notable that this explanation of the Easter and
post-Easter phenomena as not physical but metaphysical is
expressed in the New Testament more often than any other
view. Found especially in Luke, John, Acts, and the letters
of Paul, (insofar as Easter and afterwards was concerned),
this was the standard view of the disciples and the inner
circle of followers regarding Jesus' appearances on Easter
and ensuing days. Since the writings of these three or four
authors, according to who wrote Acts, comprise more than
seventy percent of the New Testament, this fourth view of
the appearances on Easter and following must be considered
very important. If it were possible to speak of a New
Testament view on the subject, this explanation comes
nearest to deserving that prestige.

This nonphysical evaluation of Jesus' post-Calvary appearances is given further weight by the fact that such phenomena continue to be reported today. A grandmother in Boxford, Massachusetts, told the author of her ordeals in supporting and raising her family of five children, with the handicap of an alcoholic husband. She said that when she got at wit's end, and the way ahead seemed blocked, Jesus would come to her, lay his hand on her shoulder, and give her courage to persevere.

A Wakefield, Massachusetts, minister reported similar experiences. Upon coming home from church discouraged on Sunday evenings, with the little response of the day, he would slump down in a livingroom chair. Then Jesus would enter the room, be seated on another chair, and together the two of them would discuss the day's events.

On South Professor Street in Oberlin, Ohio, a man was walking along one evening after dark when he heard faster footsteps following him. Soon the approaching individual drew up beside the man. Looking out of the corner of his eyes, he saw that one drawing beside him was Jesus. The two walked along side by side in silence for some moments. Then the form of Jesus moved over into the original walker, and the two became one. As a result, that man had a great religious experience.

A Catholic priest in a small isolated parish among the Alps was discouraged and decided to leave. He went to the little mountain chapel to celebrate his last mass at that place. While the priest was officiating, Jesus came forth from the altar and stood before him. Jesus said, "you may leave, but I will stay." The priest changed his mind, remained in the parish, and had an illustrious priesthood thereafter.

This is not the place to attempt an evaluation concerning the validity of such experiences. Here it must suffice simply to have recognized such phenomena as a type of religious experience. It is not surprising that, from Easter afternoon and throughout the Church's beginnings, this was the favorite way of explaining Jesus' Easter appearances.

V. The Easter Appearances were but Optic Illusions

A greatly variant view, that gained wide credence among certain branches of the Early Church, became most fully developed in Gnosticism. Gnostics believed that Christ was too divine to suffer agony and death and that he only seemed to. This belief was founded also on the concept that God could not have been so cruel as to have his only son brutally crucified on the cross. The supposition therefore

was that Jesus never was crucified. It was held that he was
not even on the cross.

The extreme form of Gnosticism was called Docetism.
Docetics developed a theology of radical dualism,
maintaining that the divine is wholly good and the physical
wholly evil. It therefore was considered inconceivable that
deity should ever have any contact with a carnal physical
body. This theology drove its adherents to conclude that
there could not have been any incarnation and that what
seemed to be the body of Jesus on the cross was but an
apparition. Of the ten books of acts of the various
apostles in the Apocryphal New Testament plus the eight
minor books of acts, all but the Acts of Paul contain
docetic ideas to greater or less degree.

The typical docetic view is expressed best in the Acts
of John, A.D. 170-180.[16] In that book John is represented
as meeting with Jesus and talking with him on the Mount of
Olives at the moment his supposed body was being crucified
across the Kidron Valley in Jerusalem. In that
conversation, Jesus is recorded as having said to John in
sections 96-101, "What now I am seen to be, that I am not
. . . John, unto the multitude below in Jerusalem I am
being crucified and pierced with lances and reeds, and gall
and vinegar is given me to drink. But unto thee I speak,
and what I speak hear thou . . . . neither am I he that is

on the cross, whom now thou seest not, but only hearest his
(or a) voice . . . . Nothing, therefore, of the things which
they will say of me have I suffered."[17]

This bodily insubstantiality of Jesus, even during the
days of his ministry, is further elucidated by John in
section 93: "Sometimes when I would lay hold on him, I met
with a material and solid body, and at other times, again,
when I felt him, the substance was immaterial and as if it
existed not at all . . . . And oftentimes when I walked with
him, I desired to see the print of his foot, whether it
appeared on the earth; for I saw him as it were lifting
himself up from the earth: and I never saw it."[18]

A variant Gnostic view was attributed to Basilides of
Alexandria, A.D. 117-118. The church father Irenaeus said
Basilides maintained that Simon of Cyrene was crucified by
mistake "and Jesus himself took the form of Simon, and stood
by and laughed at them."[19]

Extreme docetics maintained that the whole life of
Jesus was not a physical reality but only a prolonged
spiritual appearance, whatever that might be, on earth.
Since these extreme docetics regarded the flesh as material
and bad, they concluded that the spiritual Christ could not
have had any fleshly body at any time.

Although there are no docetic books in the New
Testament, many passages presumably were written to combat
Gnosticism in general. For instance, I John 1:1-3 is
insistent that Christ was "seen," "handled," "manifested,"
and "heard" among men. The same emphasis is found in 4:1-3
where it is asserted that only those are "of God" who
confess "that Jesus Christ has come in the flesh." II John
7 also refers to the docetics when it says, "For many
deceivers have gone out into the world, those men who will
not acknowledge the coming of Jesus Christ in the flesn."

The Gnostic heresy was particularly strong in Syria and
Egypt. Paul wrote parts of the early chapters in I
Corinthians against it and it infiltrated parts of the
Fourth Gospel. Its extreme element always was insistent
that Jesus had not been crucified, therefore had not died,
and consequently could not have been resurrected. His
supposed appearances on Easter day were but a grand optical
illusion.

VI. The Disciples Stole the Body of Jesus

It should be remembered that Jesus had not only friends
but also opponents in Jerusalem, and their verdict on Easter
day must be consulted. As news of the empty tomb spread
through that city it might have been expected that the

enemies of Jesus would deny that any resurrection had
occurred. They explained the empty tomb by asserting that
the disciples stole the body of Jesus.

This view is reflected in Matthew's wholly fictional
reconstruction of the entombment process where "the chief
priests and the Pharisees" are represented at that time as
fearful that such a theft might take place. To prevent such
an outcome, they are said to have approached Pilate with the
request that he make such a theft impossible. "We remember
what that deceiver said while he was yet alive. 'After
three days I will rise again.' Command, therefore, that the
sepulchre be made secure until the third day, lest perchance
his disciples come and steal him away and say to the people,
'He has risen from the dead,' and the last error will be
worse than the first" (Matthew 27:63-64). Pilate is
represented as having granted the request by sealing the
door and placing a guard around the tomb (Matthew 27:65-66).

His enemies accordingly insisted that Jesus had not
been alive on Easter day at all. His dead body, they said,
had been stolen from the tomb by the disciples for deceptive
purposes and had been spirited away to some secret tomb.
According to this view, the whole resurrection story was a
grand hoax, perpetrated upon the populace by the disciples.

Although no New Testament writer held this view, it is
reflected in the Matthean passage in question as the

explanation of the empty tomb that was held by Jesus' opponents.

VII.   No Death, Only Coma, followed by Physical Revival

According to a seventh view, Jesus never died but was only in a presumed state of coma when he was removed from the cross and was buried. Various clues in the crucifixion and entombment procedures appear to support this position.

First, Jesus died too soon. The Roman preference for crucifixion was grounded in the fact that it was the most cruel and ghastly form of execution known. Usually the victim languished in torture on the cross for three or four days before thirst, tension, and mounting bodily poisons finally brought about death. By contrast, Jesus died in only three hours. Such quick death on a cross would have been virtually unprecedented. This was so amazing tnat "Pilate marveled if he were already dead" (Mark 15:44). In that event, he would have died of heart failure rather than from crucifixion as such.

As a second bit of evidence in support of tnis view, the assertion of Jesus' being dead rested on the word of only one man, tne Roman centurion who was left to attend tne crucifixion scene. "And Pilate . . . calling unto him the centurion, asked him if he had been any while dead. And

when he learned it of the centurion, he granted the corpse
to Joseph" (Mark 15:44-45).

A third indication lies in the favorableness of the
centurion toward Jesus. This guard apparently was certain
that a great injustice had been done and that a righteous
man had been hung on the cross. "And when the centurion who
stood by over against him saw that he so gave up the ghost,
he said, 'Surely this man was a son of God,'" i.e., a godly
man (Mark 15:39). Luke interpreted this statement correctly
when he wrote, "And when the centurion saw what was done, he
glorified God, saying, 'Certainly this was a righteous man'"
(Luke 23:47). These high appraisals on the part of the
Roman centurion may well have formed the basis of some
favoritism extended to Jesus.

A fourth item to note is that Pilate also thought Jesus
was not guilty, but had been improperly condemned. "And
Pilate said to the chief priests and the multitudes, 'I find
no fault in this man'" (Luke 23:4). Pilate tried to escape
the demands of the priestly mob by sending Jesus to Herod
for decision (Luke 23:7). However, Herod refused to get
implicated in this case, and after a little mocking, sent
Jesus back to Pilate (Luke 23:8-12).

"Then Pilate called together the chief priests and the
rulers and the people, and said to them, 'You brought unto
me this man, as one who perverts the people: but behold,

having examined him before you, I have found no fault in this man concerning those things of which you accuse him -- no, nor even Herod; for he sent him back to us, and behold, nothing worthy of death has been done by him. I will therefore chastise him and release him'" (Luke 23:13-16).

When the infuriated mob cried out in protest, saying, "Away with this man" (vs. 18), "Pilate spoke to them again, desiring to release Jesus" (vs. 20). When the enraged mob finally shouted in unison, "Crucify, crucify him," Pilate continued to resist the mob pressure as "he said to them the third time, 'Why, what evil has this man done? I have found no cause of death in him. I will therefore chastise him and release him'" (vss. 21-22).

Only as the people of the mob (made up of priests, Sanhedrin members, and populace [vs. 13]) became still more raving did Pilate capitulate to them by turning Jesus over to be crucified. This shows clearly that the crucifixion was not brought about by the Romans.

Matthew similarly records that Pilate tried to release Jesus "For he knew that for envy they had delivered him up" (Matthew 27:18). It is even recorded that Pilate's wife urged him not to get implicated into executing Jesus. "And while he was sitting on the judgment-seat, his wife sent unto him, saying, 'Have nothing to do with that righteous man, for I have suffered many things this day in a dream because of him'" (Matthew 27:19).

The wild clamor of the mob for the crucifixion of Jesus finally forced Pilate to weaken in order to keep favor with the Jewish power structure of Jerusalem. "So when Pilate saw that he was achieving nothing, but rather that a mob was forming, he took water and washed his hands before the multitude, saying, 'I am innocent of the blood of this righteous man. See to it yourselves.' And all the people answered and said, 'His blood be on us and on our children'" (Matthew 27:24-25). With apparent great regret Pilate therefore finally allowed the crucifixion to take place, at 12:00 noon on that Friday.

By 3:00 p.m., when the religious elite had already disappeared to their homes to make eleventh-hour preparations for Passover, there apparently was no continuing mob remaining to exert further pressure against Jesus. Consequently, if Jesus lapsed into a state of coma, it was an invitation to his new friends to remove him from the cross at once.

Since the disciples and his other followers had long since deserted him, so that according to the Synoptics Jesus ostensibly died friendless, this was all the more reason why Joseph of Arimathea felt impelled to take action. Accordingly, he and the centurion at once secured permission from Pilate for removal of the body. Feeling that he had been unjustly crucified, the least this trio could do was to put a speedy end to having such an innocent person subjected to further shame on that cross. Since no friends were in evidence, Joseph offered his new unused sepulchre for the entombment of this forsaken person.

Under the supposition that Jesus had only gone into some form of coma, it would seem evident that his body was stimulated back to full life as the coldness of the tomb worked itself through the linen windings in which he had been enshrouded. He may well have regained consciousness long before Sunday morning but found himself securely bound in the grave clothes and unable to make his calls for help heard. This would have been particularly true on the Passover Sabbath when people were not traveling, especially to cemeteries.

It is difficult for anyone in our era of embalming to understand how commonly, in pre-embalming days, people supposedly dead came back to life after a season. In the embalming process the blood is all sucked from the body and formaldehyde, or some other preservative, is pumped into the circulatory system. After that, an individual cannot come back to life if he should wish to.

This author was brought up on evening stories of corpses being moved from one cemetery to another, with evidences that many individuals had come to life after burial. There were accounts of where people had changed position, lying face down, or curled up in the coffin, or women having pulled their hair out.

Through the years the author has had direct connection with various cases of unembalmed people who have come back to life, either shortly before or after burial. A Maine bride from a remote area died immediately after her wedding day, and so was appropriately buried in her wedding gown. As it was an exceptionally severe winter, with the ground frozen too deep for digging, she was placed in a mausoleum to await spring interment. However, as the cold of the tomb began to penetrate the coffin, she was chilled out of her coma and came back to life. She pushed up the lid of her carpenter-made coffin and crawled out. Then, finding herself locked in the mausoleum, she broke a window, and making her exit through it, walked to her nearby home through a snowstorm with her bridal veil trailing behind her.

Over the line in New Hampshire was the episode where an unembalmed wife was being buried. The funeral procession was entering the church. While ascending the steps, one of the four pallbearers stumbled and dropped his corner of the coffin so it came down with a thud. This sudden jar brought the wife inside the coffin back to life and funeral mourning was turned into the excitement of rejoicing.

The last sermon this author preached in New England was at the Congregational Church in Rowley, Massachusetts.

After services he was entertained at the home of Deacon
Jewett, the patriarch of the parish. He showed the Boston
papers that told of his death from typhoid fever, with the
announcement of his funeral services, forty years previous.
After he had been supposedly dead for more than twenty-four
hours, the family heard someone say that when people die of
typhoid fever it is sometimes possible to revive them by
dipping them into cold water. Since typhoid was the cause
of his death, the family decided to try the remedy. Living
on a New England farm, they pumped the watering trough full
of cold water from the well. Then they dropped him into
it. The sudden shock brought his heart to beating again in
normal fashion and he came out of the presumed coma into
which he had fallen. He lived on for forty more years and
that afternoon the author had the privilege of being
entertained by him.

One day in Northern Ohio the author visited the
Wyandotte Museum in Upper Sandusky. It was a rainy day,
with no other visitor in the museum. The curator, perhaps
to reward his guest who had come on such an inclement day,
said, "You may be interested in this article which came in
only yesterday." He showed a small child's coffin. The
curator said, "This was brought in yesterday by a man over
six feet tall and in his eighties who said he would have no
further use for it and wondered if the museum would care for
it."

Then the man told the story behind this small coffin. When an infant he had ostensibly died. His father drove to Upper Sandusky with horse and carriage to have a coffin made. Eventually he found a carpenter who had time to make one and the farmer waited until the article was completed. Then he drove back home with it. The next day the funeral procession of carriages formed and proceeded to the church. However, the road was bumpy and on the way the infant began to cry. So the procession turned around and went home.

Several days later the child died again. Once more family and friends proceeded, after due announcement, to the same church and cemetery. The coffin was being lowered into the grave. However, it was allowed to hit the bottom a little harder than was intended and the child began crying again. So he was taken home and did not die again. Now he was in his eighties, and surrendering his coffin as a curio of the pre-embalming age.

Only several years ago a girl was buried unembalmed in Cleveland, Ohio. After the interment people heard moanings at her grave. But these were diagnosed as the voice of the spirits who were contending for her soul. Apparently this young girl also had been buried alive.

A still more recent Cleveland case was of an orthodox Jew whose family of course would not allow embalming. This man died in the afternoon and the service was arranged for

the following day. When the funeral director came into the
mortuary the next morning to ready the corpse finally for
the service, this man, whom medical authority had pronounced
dead, was found alive and sitting up.

While this is being written (August 3, 1970) wire
reports of a similar case have just come in from Brazil.
"The funeral cortege of Jose Pereira Viana, 30, was moving
slowly towards Pendotiba Cemetery in Niteroi, Brazil, when a
young friend of the deceased asked once more to see the face
of the man with whom he had grown up. The funeral party
agreed. The lid of the coffin was removed and Viana, lying
amid the satin and flowers, yawned, rubbed his eyes and sat
up. The mourners scattered while he got out of the coffin
and asked for a cup of coffee. Viana was back at his farm
last weekend with his parents and fiancee, receiving the
congratulations of friends and neighbors."

Apparently in pre-embalming days, and today where
embalming is not practiced, a rather amazing number of
people have been buried alive, presumably unconscious from
some cause or in a state of coma. May it be that Jesus was
among this group, and revived when the cold of the tomb
worked its way through the bindings of the grave clothes?

The four types of circumstantial evidence developed
here, in support of this conclusion, would seem to carry
considerable weight. That mistakes were made often in those

days, before instruments were available to assist in accurately determining death, is quite certain. The heart-transplant movement has shown how difficult it is to determine the point of death even with instruments. Only when the verdicts from three separate examinations concur can even tne modern physician be certain death has occurred. (1) The stethoscope must reveal no breathing, (2) the cardiogram must indicate no heart action, and (3) the encephalogram must show that all brain waves have stopped.

It will be shown in Part III that, in all probability Jesus was not nailed to the cross and his side was not pierced with any spear. These two procedures are not found in the Synoptic Gospels but were later fictions devised by the author of the Fourth Gospel.

There were two good reasons why the Romans did not nail victims to the crosses in crucifixion. Most important of these, nailing victims to crosses would have punctured blood vessels, causing the victims to bleed to death quickly. This inevitability would have defeated the whole purpose of crucifixion, insuring a prolonged agonizing death.

Furthermore, it is not possible to crucify by nailing through the hands. The tendons in the hand are relatively weak so that if the body weighs more than approximately eignty-eight pounds, they will tear out and tne body will fall. Brad Lemley, reporter witn the Washington Post, has done special research in this subject. The following is his communication on this matter. "One thing we have to realize is that it's impossible to crucify a person through the hands. It's completely impossible. Some experiments were done by a physician in France in 1952 in which he took cadavers from medical school, crucified the people and found out that if you're nailed through the hands, the maximum that the body can support is 40 kilos. Anything over 40 kilos with nails through the hands, they'd simply rip out." A kilo is 2.2 pounds, making 88 pounds maximum.

Early classical Italian painters, who lived when memories of crucifixions were still vivid, painted that ordeal with the victims tied to the cross by the wrists.

All these evidences combine to show that Jesus was not nailed to the cross through his hands, and probably not through his feet. Therefore he lost no blood in the crucifixion process so that, if he were only in a state of coma, return to consciousness would have been possible. In Part III, Chapter 2, section 4 it will be shown where John got his idea that Jesus was nailed to the cross, probably the greatest deception in Christian history.

The view that Jesus was only in a state of coma when placed in the sepulchre, and that he later revived, probably will increasingly commend itself to scientifically minded modern people with advanced medical knowledge and awareness of cause and effect sequences. As such, this may be destined to be the coming view of students, scientists, and humanistic scholars.

* * * * * * *

Looking back in retrospect over this Part II, one is amazed to discover how many different views are actively expressed or reflected on the pages of the New Testament to account for the phenomena of that first Easter day. With choice among these seven explanations, everyone should be able to find his or her niche of belief. Except for the position maintained by Jesus' enemies, all of these are Christian views. With that same exception, all seven account for Jesus being alive on Easter day, either physically or metaphysically.

The dimensions of life and death are often difficult to fathom. Such determination was particularly puzzling in dealing with the complexities associated with that first Easter. Consequently, we are confronted with this variety of explanations to account for what occurred on that day of days, which to Christians has become most precious.

Notes to Part II

1. Montague R. James, The Apocryphal New Testament,
   Oxford, Clarendon Press, 2nd. impression, 1926,
   pp. 117-146.

2. ibid., II:xviii:1, pp., 123-124.

3. ibid., II:xviii:2, pp., 124-125.

4. ibid., IV:xx:1, p., 127.

5. ibid., VI:xxii:1, p., 130.

6. ibid., VI:xxii:1-2, pp., 130-131.

7. ibid., VII:xxiii:1,3. pp., 132-133.

8. ibid., VIII:xxiv, pp., 134-136.

9. ibid., IX:xxv:1, pp., 137-138.

10. ibid., IX:xxv:2, p., 139.

11. ibid., X:xxvi, p., 139.

12. ibid., XI:xxvii, p., 143.

13. ibid., pp., 166-170.

14. ibid., pp., 181-186.

15. ibid., p., 183.

16. ibid., pp., 228-270.

17. ibid., pp., 254-255.

18. ibid., pp. 252-253.

19. Haer., I.xxiv.4.

PART III

HOW THE EASTER STORY GREW FROM GOSPEL TO GOSPEL

I.

Growth in the Easter-morning Reporting

Part I gave the valid account of what happened on the
first Easter. Part II dealt with the diverse ways in which
the New Testament writers and members of the Early Church
tried to account for the occurrences of that day, especially
how to explain the appearances of Jesus. Now we embark on
Parts III and IV which reckon with the problem of growth,
how the Easter story grew from gospel to gospel and in the
thought of the Apostolic Church.

To most people today Easter is simply Easter, with
little thought except recognition of the empty tomb and that
Jesus was alive. Because so little attention is customarily
given to the intricacies of the gospel accounts, Easter
remains one of the best-kept secrets of our religion. It is
sort of a no man's land into which even most biblical
scholars do not venture. Is this reticence because they
fear that research into the events of that day may turn up
materials that may be embarrassing to their faith?

This conspiracy of silence with respect to the Easter
recordings has left Christians oblivious to the diversities
of thought with respect to those records. As the element
of growth is brougnt into the picture, it becomes evident

that the Easter story is a maze of confusions. The purpose
in this latter half of the present study is to show how the
Easter events have become rather hopelessly besmogged by
later accretions.

In spite of a lifetime of attendance at Easter
services, most people are not aware of any significant
variations between the four gospel accounts. However, a
comparative study reveals amazing differences between them.
The favorite tool in approaching gospel study is termed a
harmony of the gospels, with all three or four printed side
by side in parallel columns. Rather, such a publication
should be called "a disharmony of the gospels" because of
the wide variations and discrepancies between them which
such an arrangement makes more evident.

The three later gospels have been the victims of
accretionary growth from the time the earliest (Mark)
appeared until the latest (John) was completed. During
those three and a half decades, three types of alteration
occurred as the Easter story moved from gospel to gospel.
These changes consist in loss, gain, and modification of the
facts contained in the earliest, and presumably authentic,
reporting as found in Mark's gospel. The present chapter
will be confined to later alterations of the Easter-morning
events.

1. Change and Expansion in Luke's Rewriting

First to consider for growth is the Gospel of Luke,
produced some ten years after Mark, at approximately A.D.
75. In spite of all the good things that have been said
about Luke in previous pages, he has rather disgraced
himself in relaying to us Mark's early-morning report (Mark
16:1-8). In rewriting those eight verses Luke has made nine
significant expansions (Luke 24:1-11).

1. The number of women who came to the tomb is changed
and increased from the two Marys and Salome in Mark to the
two Marys, Joanna, "and the other women with them" (Luke
24:10/Mark 16:1).

2. By omitting "young" from Mark's "young man," Luke
not only has adultized the tomb occupant into a "man", but
thereby has lost the key to Mark's identity (Luke 24:4/Mark
16:5).

3. The one occupant in Mark is pluralized so that Luke
has "two men" in the tomb (Luke 24:4/Mark 16:5).

4. The lone tomb occupant in Mark is also supernaturalized by Luke as his "two men" become angelic beings.
This development is indicated by the women finding no one in
the tomb when suddenly these "two men" materialized and
mysteriously appeared (Luke 24:3-4/Mark 16:5). This
portrayal shows that, by the time the second gospel was

written some ten years later, the insignificant "young man"
Mark had already grown into two adult angels.

5. In Mark, the "young man" was "sitting on the right
side" while Luke's "two men stood by" the women (Luke
24:4/Mark 16:5).

6. The color of the garb was accentuated from Mark's
"clothed in a white garment" to Luke's "in dazzling
appparel" (Luke 24:4/Mark 16:5).

7. While in Mark the women made no physical reaction
to what they heard or saw except instant bolting from the
tomb, Luke has them make fitting response as "they bowed
down their faces to the ground" in proper deference to these
supernatural beings (Luke 24:5/Mark 16:5).

8. The terminus of the address to the women is
completely changed. Mark has, "But go, tell his disciples
and Peter that he is going before you into Galilee: there
you shall see him as he said to you." By contrast, Luke
has, "remember how he spoke to you when he was yet in
Galilee, saying that the Son of Man must be delivered up
into the hands of sinful men, and be crucified, and the
third day rise again." Luke completely omits Jesus'
statement that he was going to Galilee (Luke 24:7/ Mark
16:7).

9. The reaction of the women to their experience at
the tomb also became changed. Mark has, "And they went out,

and fled from the tomb, for trembling and astonishment had
come upon them: and they said nothing to anyone, for they
were terrified." Luke changed this completely into, "And
they remembered his words, and returned from the tomb, and
told all those things to the eleven, and to all the others"
(Luke 24:8-9/Mark 16:8).

These nine significant changes and amplifications show
how difficult it was to resist inroads of the popular
accretions which ten intervening years of tradition-growth
had brought. For an ordinarily reliable historian such as
Luke to have been swept off his feet into making so many
alterations, in his seven-verse rewriting of Mark's eight,
is a phenomenal development.

Since it would appear that none of Luke's nine changes
and amplifications of the Easter-morning story are
historically valid, special tribute of praise goes back to
Mark for having preserved and mediated to us the untarnished
but true record of Easter morning.

2. Matthew's Miraclizing of Easter-morning Events

If Luke was flighty in reconstructing Easter morning,
it can be said that Matthew, reflecting ten added years of
tradition-growth to A.D. 85, went wild in spectacularizing
the Easter events.

1. Mattnew made a good start even before Easter. At
the moment Jesus breathed his last breath on the cross
Mattnew states that "the earth quaked, and the rocks were
shattered, and the tombs were opened, and many bodies of the
saints who had fallen asleep were raised" (Matthew 27:51-52).

2. Matthew introduced his new group of Easter morning
spectaculars with another great earthquake. "And behold,
there was a great earthquake" which heralded a succession of
other supernatural events that he made to follow.

3. Mark in the tomb was transformed by Matthew into
"an angel of the Lord" who, in dramatic action, "descended
from Heaven, and came, and rolled away the stone, and sat
upon it" (Matthew 28:2).

4. In Matthew only the two Marys go to the sepulchre
in contrast with three named women in both Mark and Luke
(Matthew 28:1/Mark 16:1/Luke 24:10).

5. Progression in the dress of the one or two who
greeted the women is an excellent example of the story
growing from gospel to gospel. In Mark the occupant was
"clothed in a white garment." In Luke the two supernatural
beings had "dazzling apparel." Of the angel who descended
from Heaven in Matthew it is said, "His appearance was as
lightning and his raiment white as snow" (Mark 16:5/Luke
24:4/Matthew 28:3).

6. Matthew had a military garrison stationed around the sepulchre (27:62-66). He describes these soldiers as so frightened when that angel descended from Heaven like lightning, rolled the stone away, and sat on it that "for fear of him the guards quaked and became as dead men" (Matthew 28:4).

7. Instead of the women entering the tomb when they arrived, as in Mark and Luke, in Matthew the angel met them and invited them into the tomb: "Come, see the place where the Lord lay" (Matthew 28:6/Mark 16:5/Luke 24:3).

8. Mark told how the women "fled from the tomb, as trembling and astonishment had come upon them, and they said nothing to anyone, for they were terrified." Although with an echo of "fear" remaining, Matthew transformed that exit from the tomb area into a joyous experience and eagerness to tell the story to others. "And they departed quickly from the tomb, with fear and great joy, and ran to bring his disciples word" (Matthew 28:8/Mark 16:8).

9. In Mark and Luke none of Jesus' followers saw him on Easter morning, but only the hypothetical centurion. By contrast, Matthew has Jesus give an audience to the women while on their way to inform the disciples. "And behold, Jesus met them, saying 'All hail.' And they came and took hold of his feet, and worshiped him" (Matthew 28:9).

10. As a sequel to No. 1, Matthew describes an Easter
parade through Jerusalem of the saints who had been
resurrected from their tombs on Good Friday afternoon when
Jesus' last breath completed his sacrifice and brought
salvation to mankind, "and coming forth out of their tombs
after his resurrection they entered the holy city and
appeared to many" (Matthew 27:53).

Although Matthew has followed in general the Marcan-
Lucan outline of Easter-morning events, this third sketch of
those happenings is so different that it appears made from
cloth of an entirely different color. With the two great
earthquakes, rocks shattered into bits, tombs opened and
saints resurrected, spectacular descent of an angel from
Heaven like lightning, the Roman guards so petrified with
frignt that they became like dead men, procession of the
resurrected saints through the streets of Jerusalem, and
Jesus appearing to the women who worshiped him -- in all
this Matthew has created an Easter-morning scenario of
compounded miracles.

If the sun had gone down at noonday when Jesus was
nailed to the cross and it was as midnight for the three
ensuing hours, if the darkness suddenly disappeared and tne
sun returned at 3:00 p.m. when he was removed from the
cross, and if these cosmic attestations described by Matthew
had occurred on Easter morning, it would seem that, before

the day had ended, every inhabitant of Jerusalem would have become a follower of this risen Jesus for whom God had provided such spectacular endorsements.

These supposed cosmic effects have been combined by Matthew in bringing the Easter story to its highest pinnacle of elaboration. Since its innovations are evidently departures from truth, Matthew's account rates only as an Easter fantasy, describing what Easter might have been in a world of miracle.

Since the Church has loved miracle rather than factualness, Matthew's rendition has become the most-remembered Easter-morning version, the picture of the first Easter that has become normative in Christendom. This portrait is more appealing than Mark's picture of the mystified, terrified, and speechless women.

3. The Fourth Gospel's Completely New Version

If Matthew's rendition has departed from the sober recordings of Mark and Luke, John gives a radically different view of Easter morning in his chapter 20. Except in the vaguest manner, the whole synoptic outline is abandoned. The author of the Fourth Gospel has virtually thrown all three Synoptic Gospels into the wastebasket. Gone are Mark's "young man" in the tomb, Jesus' message

about going to Galilee, and the women leaving the tomb in
fright and saying nothing to anyone. John has begun all
over again at creating an almost wholly new Easter-morning
plot that was more to his liking.

This author of the Fourth Gospel seems to have realized
that the tremendous Easter buildup in Matthew was
fictitous. John refused to have anything therefore to do
with that high tower of Easter blocks. This aversion to
untruth apparently caused him to react against the beginning
of miraclizing in Luke and the tremendous buildup of cosmic
demonstrations in Matthew, all of which John avoided.

With the other women ruled out of the picture, Mary
Magdalene occupies the spotlight of attention as the
mistress of ceremonies in all the Easter-morning
proceedings. After a night of presumed sleepless concern
over Jesus, she is portrayed at the tomb alone "early, while
it was yet dark." The resurrection already had taken place,
as she found the stone rolled away and the tomb empty.

Instead of "trembling" with "astonishment" and
"fright," and saying nothing to anyone, as in Mark, Mary
Magdalene is portrayed in this gospel as totally composed
and unafraid. She "ran" at once and reported the emptied
tomb to "Simon Peter and the other disciple whom Jesus
loved" saying, "They have taken the Lord out of the tomb and
we do not know where they have laid him" (John 20:1-2).

John 20:3-10 reflects favoritism for John, who usually
is referred to in this gospel as "the disciple whom Jesus
loved," over Peter, the rash disciple. Peter was revered in
Rome and John in Ephesus. The author of the Fourth Gospel
could not allow Peter the prestige of being the only
disciple at the tomb, as reported in Luke 24:34. Therefore,
this Fourth Gospel amended that episode by having Peter and
"the disciple whom Jesus loved" going to the tomb together.
In this reconstruction, Peter is largely disparaged in favor
of John.

This gospel portrays the mood of extreme urgency on
Easter morning, with Mary Magdalene "running" to inform
Peter and John (John 20:1). These two disciples also are
represented as "running both together" to reach the tomb at
the earliest possible moment.

John, presumably "the other disciple" (John 20:4), more
sensitive to the urgency of the situation, and with the
greater zeal, is represented as outrunning Peter and
arriving at the tomb first. "Stooping and looking in he saw
the linen cloths lying" but he had such reverence for what
had occurred there that "he did not enter in" (John 20:5).

When brash Peter arrived, he irreverently barged into
the tomb and, ostensibly with doubts, glanced at the
disheveled grave clothes (John 20:6-7). After reminding
the reader again that John had arrived first, it is recorded

that, in his greater modesty and reverence, this beloved disciple finally entered the tomb. Implying that Peter was incredulous, the dialogue ends by praising John's greater spiritual discernment as it is stated that "he saw and believed" (John 20:8).

This reconstruction of the supposed race to the tomb reflects the rivalries between the Petrine and Johannine factions of the Early Church in graphic manner, showing how human nature and favoritism for preferred church leaders became woven even into the fabric of the Easter tapestry.

A revealing note is appended to the dialogue: "For as yet they did not know the Scripture that he must rise again from the dead" (John 20:9). This notation reflects the truth that Jesus never had predicted his resurrection to the disciples.

As Peter and John returned to their abodes, this gospel author focuses his spotlight upon Mary Magdalene who is said to have remained at the tomb alone, weeping (John 20:10-11). The emerging scene begins with her standing outside, weeping over the loss of her Lord.

When she looked inside she was amazed at seeing "two angels in white, sitting where the body of Jesus had lain, one at the head and one at the feet. They said to her, 'Woman, why are you weeping?' She said to them, 'Because they have taken away my lord, and I do not know where they have laid him'" (John 20:12-13).

The mysterious appearance of these two angels in an
otherwise empty tomb is reminiscent of their same instant
presence in Luke 24:4. However, here they give an entirely
different address as they are made to fit into the dialogue
style of address, so typical of the Fourth Gospel. The
angels said, "Woman, why are you weeping?" She replied, as
earlier to Peter and John, "They have taken away my Lord and
I do not know where they have laid him" (John 20:2, 13).

At that point the harsh tomb area is transformed into
an exotic Oriental garden. The Easter climax in the Fourth
Gospel occurs when Mary, while weeping, is approached by an
individual whom she supposed to be the gardener. Turning
around, "she beheld Jesus standing, but she did not
recognize that it was Jesus" (John 20:14).

Immediately a dialogue ensued as Jesus said to her,
"Woman, why do you weep? Whom do you seek?" Still assuming
that she was speaking to the gardner, she replied, "Sir, if
you have taken him away, tell me where you have laid him,
and I will take him away" (John 20:15).

As the aura of garden beauty exerts its full thrust,
that moment of confrontation is represented as so intense
that each is said to have exchanged only one word each. He
said "Mary," and she recognized him. She, in turn, said
"Rabboni (my teacher)" (John 20:16).

Jesus then is credited with a final message to Mary:
"Do not touch me, for I have not yet ascended to the Father,
but go to my brethren and say to them, I am ascending to my
Father and your Father, my God and your God." After this
brief adieu, Mary Magdalene is represented as presumably
rushing to the disciples and saying, "I have seen the Lord,"
and she told them what he had said (John 20:17-18).

* * * * * * *

This has been an enlightening odyssey, seeing how the
Easter-morning story has grown from gospel to gospel. It
was seen that Luke began this departure by making modest
changes, how Matthew added his array of miracles, with the
most radical departures and grand climax in the Fourth
Gospel as the Easter-morning story was completely
rewritten. Disagreements among these three expanded
versions are the most decisive evidences against their
veracity. Disappointing though it may seem, one is driven
back to the Gospel of Mark as having the only presumably
accurate information concerning what occurred on Easter
morning. Nevertheless, enlargement of the Easter-morning
story, with its fictional embroiderings, will continue to
attract all who love miracle rather than fact, and fancy
rather than reality.

II.

Elaboration in Rewriting the Easter-night Events

In chapter I it was observed how the Easter-morning
story grew from gospel to gospel. Since the evening
experiences in the upper room were more routine and less
startling, they never have attracted much attention.
Consequently, there has been much less amplification of
those proceedings as mediated by Mark and Luke. What growth
did take place does not consist, as with the Easter-morning
elaboration, in modifying the basic facts or pyramiding them
into miracles. Rather, additions to the Easter-night
recording consist largely of two types. (1) Jesus'
valedictory address that evening became greatly inflated
with spurious statements. (2) John has tripled that meeting
by adding two presumably fictitious post-Easter gatherings
with the disciples.

1. Mark's Gospel: First Edition

The first edition of Mark's gospel, by eyewitnesses
Mary Magdalene and her son, contained probably the only
completely authentic written record of the Easter-night
gathering in the upper room. However, as pointed out in
Part I, that ending has been removed from Mark's gospel.

Thereby, the best portrayal of Easter night has been lost.
One may guess that it told also of Jesus' final hours in
Jerusalem. That original ending probably was removed
because it was not sufficiently miraculous to satisfy the
emerging Church. Since that original has been lost, it
unfortunately is not available, as the master morning
report, for measuring the extent of growth in later gospels.

2. Blank-Out in Matthew's Gospel

Since there was no record of an Easter-night gathering
in the truncated Gospel of Mark, ending at 16:8, which
evidently was at Matthew's disposal, he knew of no meeting
late that evening in the upper roon. Consequently, Matthew
made no mention of any such assembly.

3. Luke's Salvage of Mark's Easter-night Recording

Part I, Fifth Report, has shown how Luke salvaged the
Easter-night report from the first edition of Mark's
gospel. Luke 24:33-49 therefore is the most authentic
account of Easter evening that has survived.

Although Part I has rated him next to Mark in the
accuracy of reporting, Luke was by no means a perfect
recorder. In the previous chapter it was shown that in
transcribing the eight verses of Easter-morning report in

Mark 16:1-8 Luke made nine rather significant errors of change or expansion in his corresponding verses (Luke 24:1-10). Nevertheless, from the consistency in unfavorably portraying the group on Easter evening, one can guess that Luke transcribed Mark's record of the occurrences on that night without appreciable change (Luke 24:36-49). It portrays a frightened, disillusioned, and unbelieving group. When Jesus appeared among them, they feared him, refused to touch him, and virtually ignored him.

Even though the Marcan original for Easter Evening is not available for comparison, certain exceptions can be made to Luke's transcribing. One is struck at once by two apparent inaccuracies in listing the greeting given by the upper-room company to the Emmaus pair as they entered: "The Lord has indeed risen and has appeared to Simon" (Luke 24:34).

1. Such a jubilant greeting could hardly have come from the people who, throughout that day and in the following verses 36-43, were so depressed.

2. The statement that Peter saw Jesus is untrue as neither Peter nor any one of the inner circle of disciples or women saw Jesus during the daylight hours on Easter day. Although Peter went to the sepulchre, he found only the empty tomb (Luke 24:12). Of the whole inner circle it is recorded, "but they did not see him" (Luke 24:24).

3. Presumed error also consisted in supplementing Jesus' speech with a statement which he probably did not give: "And he said to them, 'Thus it is written that the Christ (Messiah) should suffer and rise again from the dead the third day'" (Luke 24:46).

There are three objections to the authenticity of this statement. First, Jesus considered himself a prophet and not the political Messiah (Christ) who would win independence for Palestine. Second, there is no Scripture in the Old Testament which predicts that the Messiah (Christ) would be crucified and rise from the dead in three days. Third, the reactions of his inner circle of disciples and women on Easter day show that, as dealt with at length in Part II, Jesus had never made to them any prediction that he would be crucified and rise from the dead in three days.

4. A minor flaw consists in Luke's statement that Jesus commissioned the disciples to go out and preach "repentance and remission of sins" (Luke 24:47). While Part II has shown that the repentance element is correct, Jesus did not preach remission of sins. His whole concern was on repentant living rather than on getting sins removed.

In spite of these four minor exceptions, Luke's reporting of the Easter-night meeting stands as a piece of near-perfect reporting, with only these minor supplements to the Marcan presumed authentic original. Since Luke's portrait of Easter night is the nearest to complete truth that has survived the ages, the task now is, using this record as a basis, to see how the Easter-night story has grown in the two later gospel endings.

4. Complete Reconstruction by John

This gospel, coming considerably later at approximately A.D. 100, shows the greatest amount of growth, if such it may be called. Although following the Lucan outline of those night events in general (Luke 24:33-49), the eleven verses of John 20:19-29 register so many changes and additions that it becomes virtually a completely new Easter-night account, reconstructed as freely as he did with the Easter-morning events.

1. John has the doors to the upper room "locked . . . for fear of the Jews" (John 20:19). This did not deter Jesus from entering, presumably miraculously going through a closed door.

2. In Luke 24:39 Jesus invited the company to feel his hands and feet, the exposed parts of his body, that he was a flesh and bones person and not a spirit body or ghost. "See my hands and my feet, that it is I myself. Handle me, and see, for a spirit does not have flesh and bones as you behold me having." By contrast, John 20:20 has Jesus show

the nail and spear wounds as "he showed them his hands and his side." As there is no nailing or spearing in the other three gospels, and as Part II has shown that Romans tied their victims to crosses and did not nail or spear them, it is evident that John has missed tne point of showing hands and feet and instead made the act into a display of supposed crucifixion wounds. That the two men on the Emmaus Road on Easter afternoon did not recognize Jesus shows that he had no nailwounds in nis hands and feet (Luke 24:13-32). Jesus' round-trip walk to Emmaus and return on that afternoon probably woula have been impossible if his feet had three-day-old nail wounds which by then would likely have been badly infected.

3. "The disciples therefore were glad when they saw the Lord" in John 20:20 is in sharp contrast to the Lucan parallel in which they were frightened, petrified, dumfounded, and unbelieving. Here John was reconstructing the evening as it should have oeen rather than portraying it as it was.

4. John preserves the actual salutation, but in verse 21 he has Jesus needlessly repeat it: "Peace be unto you."

5. Instead of simply urging the disciples to go out and continue his mission, John has Jesus formally commission them: "As the Father has sent me, so I send you" (John 20:21).

6. Instead of advising the disciples to remain in Jerusalem until they could recover from their discouragement and regain some of God's spirit and power before going forth on their new mission, as in Luke 24:49, John 20:22 has this entire transformation take place in a moment as "he breathed upon them and said to them 'Receive ye the Holy Spirit.'" According to this gospel Jesus' followers did not need to wait until Pentecost to receive the Holy Spirit.

7. John also has innovated radically by having Jesus formally institute the Catholic confessional there in the upper room before his departure. He is made to transform his disciples into priests as he said, "Whose soever sins you forgive, they are forgiven unto them; and whose soever sins you retain, they are retained" (John 20:23). Thereby the antipriestly synoptic Jesus is transformed into the great high priest who ordains his subordinates.

8. John ruled out the women and the Emmaus pair from the night session and transformed that chaotic and divisive gathering into a virtually formal planning session.

9. Thomas, a nondescript disciple never mentioned in the Synoptic Gospels except in lists, is placed under the spotlight of attention in John. In John 11:16 he is made to express the wish that he might die with Jesus and in 14:5 is credited with having inspired Jesus' master address beginning "I am the way, the truth, and the life." By the

date the Fourth Gospel was written, Thomas had become the idol of the heretical Gnostic movement which was flourishing in the churches of Egypt and Syria.

Since the Fourth Gospel has a strain of Gnosticism, Thomas is featured especially in the Easter-night overtone. Because the disciples performed so disgracefully on Easter night, tne Fourth Gospel shields Thomas from that onus by declaring that he was not present (John 20:24). The implication is that things would have gone quite differently if he had been there. His reputed absence is refuted by Luke 24:33 which specifically lists all eleven disciples as present.

10. When Thomas, represented as the model of eagerness and thoroughness, learned of Jesus' having been present on Easter night, this disciple is made virtually to reprove the others for their superficial observation and not having examined Jesus more carefully. Thomas is quoted as naving said to the other disciples, "Except I shall see in his hands the print of the nails, and put my finger into the print of the nails, and put my hand into his side, I will not believe" (John 20:25).

11. In Luke there is only one session of Jesus after Calvary with his followers, in the upper room on Easter night. John multiplied this by two, staging a second night meeting with the disciples eight days later, presumably so Thomas could be present.

12. Again Jesus entered miraculously, apparently
through the locked doors (vs. 26).

13. Of all the disciples, Jesus is represented as
having honored Thomas to the extent of speaking only to him
on that evening (John 20:27-29).

14. According to the Fourth Gospel the main purpose of
the second upper-room meeting with the disciples was to make
"a believer" out of Thomas by having him stick his finger
into the supposed nail holes and place his hand in the
assumed spear-wound in Jesus' side. Jesus is made to
respond to Thomas' request by saying, "Reach hither your
finger and see my hands and reach hither your hand and put
it into my side, and be not faithless, but believing" (John
20:27). Upon following these directives Thomas is portrayed
as shouting, "My Lord and my God" (vs. 28).

It already has been pointed out in section 7 of Part II
that Jesus neither was nailed to the cross nor had his side
pierced. Consequently, there were no nail or spear wounds
to probe. These are but fictions which have intruded
themselves into the Fourth Gospel, and only there. The
nailing and spearing evidently were derived by John from
Psalm 22:16 (17 in Hebrew) and Zechariah 12:10 under the
erroneous supposition that those passages were prophetically
describing the crucifixion of Jesus, and under the further
assumption that the crucifixion procedures followed those

prophecies meticulously. Since this process of reasoning is now seen to be wholly fallacious, and there is no support for nailing or side stabbing in the Synoptic Gospels, it is fairly certain that these can be dismissed as later fictions.

15. The prestige of Thomas is further heightened by the fact that in this gospel the final summation of the evening was addressed only to him: "Because you have seen me, you have believed: blessed are they who have not seen, and yet have believed" (John 20:29).

Undue attention to Thomas, as the only named disciple on Jesus' two night sessions with them, was probably to convince the Gnostics, who did not believe in a physical resurrection, that Jesus did return physically from the tomb.

16. John has a clever way of surmounting the expectation of Christ's second coming, which has been such a pestiferous doctrine from that day to the present. On Easter morning Jesus is recorded as saying to Mary Magdalene, "Touch me not, for I have not yet ascended to the Father" (John 20:17). By contrast, one week after Easter Jesus is represented as inviting Thomas to put his finger into the nailwounds and "reach hither your hand and put it into my side" (John 20:27). By having both the ascension and second coming occur during the week after Easter John evidently thought he had disposed of belief in a second coming for all time to come.

These sixteen changes and additions in the course of
eleven verses show how radically John revised the Easter-
night story, adding a hypothetical eighth-day overtone.
With this he completed his gospel, adding only a brief
postscript stating that "many other things" might have been
included, and ending with a statement of the gospel's
purpose, "that believing, you may have life in his
(Christ's) name" (John 20:31).

5. Third Meeting with Disciples in Fourth-Gospel Appendix

A second hypothetical overtone of the Easter-night
meeting has been added to this gospel as an appendage in
chapter 21. It describes a meeting between Jesus and seven
of his disciples at daybreak on the shores of the Sea of
Galilee. This episode is so different from the valid
Easter-night story that a point by point listing of con-
trasts would be unfruitful. The chapter is really a post-
Easter mosaic made up by combining certain episodes from
Jesus' ministry: the miraculous draught of fishes, the
storm and walking on the water, the loaves and fishes in the
Sermon on the Mount, and Peter's triple denial of Jesus at
his trial.

This appendix also pinpoints the rivalry between the
followers of Peter and the followers of John. Since this

gospel supplement was written by one from the latter group,
Peter is put at a disadvantage throughout.

1. Peter is represented as first to desert Christ's
mission as he is quoted as having said, "I am going
fishing." This supposed prince of the apostles bears the
further onus of leading the other disciples to desert the
cause with him and revert to their old vocations on the Sea
of Galilee (John 21:3).

2. Peter apparently was the only disciple who was so
immodest as to fish in the nude (John 21:7).

3. Jesus came to the disciples, presumably, to reprove
Peter and his associates for deserting the cause. Peter did
not recognize Jesus when he appeared. It took the disciple
"whom Jesus loved" to point out to Peter that this was "the
Lord" (vs. 7).

4. Peter is reminded that his father had the revered
"John" name, suggesting Peter's degeneracy (vs. 15).

5. Jesus insinuated (vs. 15) that Peter had more
regard for the 153 species of fish, taken in his marvelous
catch, than for his religious leader: "Do you love me more
than these?"

6. Peter evidently had not realized that Jesus was
responsible for the miraculous draught of fish.

7. By putting to Peter the question "Do you love me?"
three times, Jesus was twitting this disciple triply for

having denied him three times during his trial (John
21:14-17). Peter apparently was too dull to recognize tne
analogy and so was irked by the triple repetition.

8. Peter also was annoyed by the triple repetition of
the directive "Feed my lambs" or "Feed my sheep." Even with
three repetitions it is apparent that Peter is represented
as not comprehending what Jesus was saying (John 21:15-17).

9. Thickheaded Peter had to be told twice to "Follow
me" (John 21:19, 22).

10. When John turned to follow Jesus, Peter
represented it and said in a disparaging mood, "Lord, and
what will this man do?" Jesus, agitated, told Peter to mind
his own affairs and get on with his own apostleship, "What
is that to you? Follow thou me" (John 21:21-22).

11. Muddled Peter got the misconception that Jesus had
promised John exemption from death, and Peter expressed nis
resentment to Jesus. Jesus denied having made any such
promise and advised Peter again to mind his own affairs
(John 21:23). "If I wish that he tarry till I come, what is
that to you?"

In these eleven ways chapter 21 of John has snown Peter
to have been a thoroughly ridiculous person. By contrast,
John is portrayed as "the disciple whom Jesus loved" (vss.
7 & 20) "who also leaned back on nis breast at the supper
and said, 'Lord, who is he who is betraying you?'"

It is tragic that John of Ephesus, presumed author of
the Fourth Gospel, should have appended chapter 21 as an
afterthought, defaming Peter further and thereby the Petrine
segment of the Church by registering this antipathy as a
second overtone to the Easter-night experience. The further
indignity lay in adding the notation, "we know that his
witness is true" (John 21:24).

It would seem doubtful that there is any truth to
John's triple expansion of the Easter-night appearance by
adding the ones eight days later and finally by the Sea of
Galilee. However, they reveal the jockeying for position
among leaders of the Early Church and illustrate the fact
that there is much human nature in the Bible.

6.   Two New Endings to Mark's Gospel

The number of manuscripts of Mark's gospel that end at
16:8 indicate that it circulated for years in that truncated
form. In the course of time one or more individuals who
came to realize that this gospel had lost its ending, set
about to supply what presumably had been excised from that
gospel's conclusion. The resultant false ending in Mark
16:9-20 is presented as the supposed latter portion of
Jesus' speech on Easter evening in the upper room and is
included today in most of our Bibles. However, the better

Bibles, such as the Revised Standard Version, print the addition in fine type to suggest that it is not in the best manuscripts.

The resultant appendix appears to be the work of two authors. Author A, to whom one can assign Mark 16:9-15, made an honest attempt at reconstructing what occurred at the Easter-night meeting. It is mostly a modest rewriting of Luke's record, with only a slight amount from John.

1. Verse 9 follows John 20:1, 11-18 in dispensing with the other women and making Jesus glorify Mary Magdalene by meeting her in the garden alone on Easter morning.

2. Verses 10-11, telling that Mary Magdalene informed the disciples of Jesus' being alive and that they "disbelieved" comes from Luke 24:8-11 and John 20:18, but that they "mourned and wept" is likely an untrue expansion.

3. Verses 12-13 about Jesus' appearance to the two men on the Emmaus road, and their report to Jerusalem, is an extremely terse but true summary of Luke 24:13-35.

4. Verse 14, although a little strong in having Jesus "upbraid" the disciples at the evening meal, is a summary of Luke 24:36-42 and John 20:19-29.

5. Verse 15, recording what commonly is termed "The Great Commission," is a compacted summary of Luke 24:47, Matthew 28:19-20, and John 20:21. The author of this verse followed faithfully his three sources, not knowing that they

had not rendered the underlying Aramaic words of Jesus
properly into Greek at this point. The key word here, with
consonants a-r-ts, carries the triple meaning of earth,
world, or land. Since it is pretty certain that Jesus did
not have any concept of initiating a world mission, his
words, as recorded in this Marcan annex might more properly
be rendered into English as, "And he said to them, 'Go
throughout the whole land (of Palestine) and preach the
Gospel to every ethnic group.'" Luke retained this meaning
in his use of the Greek word etnne. Jesus was requesting
that his disciples extend their ministry to the whole land
of Palestine, including virtually untouched Judaea, and
preach to every ethnic group, including Samaritans, Syrians,
Lebanese, and any other foreigners who might be sojourning
in Palestine, and every social and economic class. This was
his Great Commission.

      If condensation was desired, the person who is here
called Author A has done a marvelous job of compacting the
entire Easter story into seven short verses. He was uncanny
in avoiding the untrue expansions and the miraculous in his
gospel sources. The only exception is in his following
John's gospel in having Mary Magdalene alone at the tomb and
seeing Jesus on Easter morning. His restoration gave to
Mark's gospel again a worthy ending, concluding in a climax
with the Great Commission.

An individual whom we shall call Author B evidently was dissatisfied with the new Marcan ending and decided to append one of his own. He proceeded with unrestrained abandon at having a field day of attributing unworthy valedictory statements to Jesus on Easter night. These supposed ultimate admonitions are false to the religion of Jesus and amount to a paganizing of Christianity (Mark 16:16-18).

1. "He who believes and is baptized shall be saved" (Mark 16:16) is too easy a religion. While here salvation can be secured in a few moments of resolve and performing a simple ritual, for Jesus' salvation is dependent upon a lifetime of godly living.

2. Baptism was not a part of Jesus' religion. In the Synoptic Gospels neither Jesus nor his disciples ever baptized anyone. Although he was immersed in the Jordan, Jesus apparently reacted against water baptism as a crude primitivism and materialism that has no place in spiritual religion. For water gods to wash away one's sins was too naive a religious concept. Over this issue Jesus broke relations with John the Baptist. This notation comes from an Early Church which had introduced baptism on Pentecost.

3. In verse 17 Jesus is made to say, "And these signs shall accompany those who believe in my name." A New Testament "sign" is a miracle that is done in order to prove

that what the performer does or says is acceptable to God.
Jesus is credited throughout the Gospel of John with "signs"
to prove his sonship.

By contrast, in the Synoptic Gospels Jesus was
nauseated by the clamor of the people that he perform
"signs" so they could believe in him. In his synoptic
ministry he never performed a "sign" to commend himself or
his message. He said, "This generation is an evil
generation. It seeks after a sign, but no sign shall be
given to it except the sign of Jonah. For even as Jonah
became a sign unto the Ninevites, so shall be the son of man
to this generation" (Luke 11:29-30). The only sign Jonah
needed was the Ninevite repentance that followed his
preaching. Similarly, Jesus said that the only sign he
needed to cite was the widespread spiritual awakening which
his ministry was producing. This was a nonmiraculous sign,
the transformation of people into a higher level of
spiritual life.

It therefore is the height of absurdity to find this
Author B contradicting Jesus on this point by asserting that
every believer should be able to perform five types of signs:

a. Casting out demons. Jesus is made to command his
followers to drive out demons. Old Testament religion
already had risen above belief in demons. The amazing
resurgence of demonology in New Testament time plagued Jesus

throughout his ministry when all mental disorders were popularly thought to be caused by indwelling demons. In light of Jesus' monotheistic belief, it is doubtful if he would have listed "casting out demons" as a top priority in religion.

b. Speaking in other tongues. Since neither Jesus nor his disciples ever indulged in such dubious religious expression in the gospels, it seems doubtful that he would have prescribed this pestiferous practice as the second priority in religion. Starting with the Pentecost mob, and becoming endemic in Paul's Corinth, he had to mute the movement by declaring it the least worthy of all types of religious practice. Jesus would hardly have sanctioned, let alone prescribed, this illiterate type of religious expression where unintelligible babbling is rated as the highest of spiritual gifts.

c. Handling serpents without any ill effects from their venom. A new low consisted in making Jesus institute snake handling as one of the five basic tests of true religion. It is idiotic that any individual could have advanced this view, so manifestly false, that Christians are exempt from the effects of snake venom, turning religion into a snake cult.

d. Drinking "any deadly" poison with "no hurt" to the drinker. The ultimate travesty on Jesus lies in having him

prescribe ordeal by poison as an infallible test of
religion. Like snake handling, this practice also is MURDER.

e. Being able to "lay hands on the sick" and have them
recover. This also is a dubious test of religion, as all
people die of some malady, with no response from prayers or
"laying on of hands" or anointing. This directive also
becomes a prescription for death by giving the impression
that prayers of the faithful for healing always are
answered, and in virtually ordering "believers" to avoid
medicines, doctors, surgery, and hospitals.

The onesidedness of this supposed valedictory
quinquelogue on the lips of Jesus as his final directives at
his last presence with the disciples on Easter night is seen
in the fact that four of the five deal with matters of
health, and in a destructive manner. What a travesty on
Jesus that the Gospel of Mark is made to end with this
complex of religious lies placed on the lips of Jesus.

If the barrier between Jesus and his disciples on
Easter night had become bridged so he could speak reasonably
to them, it would seem he would have spent that
strategically valuable time pleading for their enduring
loyalty to the fundamental principles of religion as ne had
enunciated them in his Sermon on the Mount.

* * * * * * *

This search began with a presumably authentic record:
Mark's description of Easter morning and Luke's salvaging of
Mark's expurgated recounting of Easter afternoon, evening,
and night. Digression from fact began with Luke's
unwarranted changes and additions in transcribing Mark's
report of Easter morning. The great mushrooming took place
when Matthew miraclized and supernaturalized the Easter
morning occurrences into spectacular manifestations.
Unhindered by facts, John wove an entirely new tapestry of
Easter events, placing only Mary at the tomb, and in
dialogue with Jesus, plus tripling the Easter night of Jesus
with his disciples. This marathon of growth ended as two
interpolators added short conclusions to the truncated
Marcan gospel, one slandering Jesus by placing false
valedictory remarks on his lips.

This research has shown that the Easter story
experienced tremendous growth in moving from gospel to
gospel. With a slight departure in Luke, all the supposed
Easter recordings in Matthew, John, and the false Marcan
ending are unhistorical. This means that most of the gospel
materials about the first Easter are spurious. The tragedy
of the situation is that the historical nucleus has been
overshadowed and almost buried under the avalanche of the
later-added more spectacular recordings and miracles that
are untrue and misleading.

III.

The Ultimate Growth Miracle, the Ascension

The Easter spectaculars supplied in the gospels,
particularly Matthew's, were climaxed by the ultimate
miracle. This concerns the disposition of Jesus' corpse.
That type of predicament always arises with the death of a
religious leader who, in the course of time, comes to be
revered as a divine being.

What became of Jesus' body provides the most notable
chapter in the story of gospel growth. It began with the
probable disposition of his mortal remains in the customary
manner of that day, as described in Parts I and II.
However, as the theology about Jesus advanced from
considering him a teacher in Israel's succession of prophets
to regarding him as a deity descended from Heaven, the
Church must have found itself in jeopardy over this
situation.

On the other hand, the original ending to Mark's gospel
probably contained the truthful account of Jesus' eventual
death and entombment. It proved relatively easy to
eliminate this source of predicament by censoring off that
original ending from all extant manuscripts. In the course
of a few years, even the memory of what that lost ending
contained was likely forgotten.

On the other hand, there must have been the remaining
corpse, and then the bones of Jesus. It matters little
whether the Jerusalem ossuary referred to in Parts I and II,
with the label, "Jesus, Son of Joseph," actually contains
the bones of our Jesus or not. Whatever the details,
survival of Jesus' mortal remains likely proved a source of
major embarrassment to those segments of the Early Church
which had come to think of Jesus as God's Son sent down to
earth, or even God himself by way of "the incarnation." How
could it be that either deity had died and that his
followers had been left with his body, and then his bones?
This would indeed have been the death of God with a vengance.

Apparently two options were open to the Church to
escape from this dilemma. The first way out was to destroy
the mortal remains of their leader. However, it appears
likely that this expedient was not used.

As another option, the Early Church could ignore that
the bones of Jesus continued to exist. Even this physical
survival probably was no deterrent to the mounting theology
of the day since his ossuary likely was soon lost among the
multitude of others in the charnel houses of that day.

After almost fifty years of wrestling over this
predicament, the conclusion to Luke's gospel, at
approximately A.D. 75, surmounted this hurdle to the
satisfaction of the Apostolic Church. Undeterred by the

survival of Jesus' bodily residue, at such late date that gospel writer unveiled the fiction, which had emerged through the course of five previous decades, that Jesus had ascended to Heaven.

In advancing this assertion there were ample precedents among other religions, and even in the Old Testament itself. Unusually revered religious leaders were thought to have been transported to Heaven to escape death. At times they were taken on an exploratory visit to Heaven and were then returned to earth, as in the case of the Sumerian hero Gilgamesn. The procession of those individuals who are supposed to have escaped death by ascending bodily to Heaven provides a notable list.

ENOCH, great-grandfather of Noah, "walked witn God, and he was not, for God took him" (Genesis 5:21-24). Sirach says, "Enoch pleased the Lord, and was translated, an example of repentance to all generations . . . . No man was created on the earth such as was Enoch, for he was taken up from the earth" (Ecclesiasticus 44:16; 49:14). Enoch is honored in the New Testament also as the first individual who ascended to Heaven: "By faith Enoch was translated that he should not see death, and he was not found, for God translated him, for he had witness borne to him that before nis translation he had been well-pleasing to God" (Hebrews 11:5).

Enoch inspired later authors to produce two bodies of literature: Enoch and The Book of the Secrets of Enoch. These volumes describe Enoch's experiences in the overworld and his observations regarding the structure and laws of the universe.[1] "And . . . during his lifetime . . . he was raised aloft on the chariots of the spirit."[2]

ZIUSUDRA, hero of the flood in the Sumerian story, for saving humanity was given by the heavenly deities "Life like a god" and "Breath eternal like a god" and was transported to Dilmun, abode of the gods.[3]

ABRAHAM, according to assertion in the intertestament book The Testament of Abraham, was transported to Heaven in angelic chariots on a cloud to show him mankind's world from the heavenly perspective. However, he was returned to earth and after a time died.

MOSES, in intertestament thought was regarded as having escaped death by being transported to Heaven alive. The original Assumption of Moses, and notes to the surviving book by that name, attests to that emergent belief.[4] That Moses was thought to have come down from Heaven to confer with Jesus on the Mount of Transfiguration shows that the belief was well established by New Testament days.[5]

ELIJAH, in a "chariot of fire" drawn by "horses of fire . . . went up by a whirlwind into heaven" according to II Kings 2:11. Sirach praised Elijah "Who was taken up in a

tempest of fire, in a chariot of fiery horses"[6] His abode
thereafter in Heaven was indicated by his coming down also
to join in the Transfiguration consultation.[5]

ISAIAH, in an intertestament writing, is reputed to
have been carried up into the seventh Heaven where he
obtained a vision of God himself. Thereafter this prophet
was returned to earth.[7]

EZRA, "before he was taken up" in II Esdras 8:19 shows
the belief that Ezra also ascended to Heaven after his work
on earth was completed.

Rabbinical literature asserts that even minor Old
Testament characters were rewarded, for specific acts of
meritorious service, by escaping death through being taken
alive to Heaven:

ELIEZER, Abraham's faithful steward.

EBED-MELECH, for saving Jeremiah's life (Jeremiah
38:7ff.).

HIRAM, King of Tyre, for his friendship to King Solomon.

JABEZ, for favoring Israel (I Chronicles 4:10).

SERAH, in Genesis 46:17, and

PHARAOH'S DAUGHTER, for saving Moses.[8]

Such are the accounts of Jewish-Christian religious
leaders who were believed to have escaped death by ascending
to Heaven. The same is found also in other religious
traditions where those especially highly regarded were

thought to have gone directly to the celestial religions.[9] Guides at the Dome of the Rock in Jerusalem tell how Muhammed on horseback on Mount Moriah was carried up to Heaven, horse and all, with such vigor that he was taking the whole mountain with him. To prevent this his followers grabbed hold of the mountain and pulled it back to earth.

Against this background of widespread ascensionism, and the greatness his followers attributed to Jesus, it would have been remarkable if the tradition had not developed that he ended his ministry with God's favoring him by ascension to Heaven.

The falsity of this ascension claim is revealed in the discrepancies between the various accounts with respect to both the time and place it supposedly occurred. The ascension furnishes another classic illustration of how the Easter story grew.

The spurious ending which has been attached to later manuscripts of Mark's gospel in 16:9-20 gives the impression that the ascension of Jesus took place from the upper room in Jerusalem at approximately midnight on Easter day, immediately following his short benedictory talk with the disciples. "So then, the Lord Jesus, after he had spoken to them, was received up into Heaven and sat down at the right hand of God" (Mark 16:19).

The Gospel of Luke agrees with Mark in respect to timing but places the ascension at a different location, considerably east of Jerusalem in the town of Bethany. "And he led them out as far as Bethany. Then he raised his hands and blessed them. And it happened, while he was blessing them, he parted from them and was carried up to Heaven. And they worshiped him and returned to Jerusalem with great joy" (Luke 24:50-52).

The Book of Acts differs from all the gospels in most fundamental respects as it describes "the day in which he was received up, after he had given commandment through the Holy Spirit to the apostles whom he had chosen, to whom he also showed himself alive after his passion by many proofs, appearing to them for the duration of forty days and speaking the things concerning the kingdom of God. And . . . as they were looking, he was taken up and a cloud received him out of their sight. . . . Then they returned to Jerusalem from the mount called Olivet which is distant from Jerusalem a Sabbath day's journey off" (Acts 1:2-3, 9, 12).

This Acts version of the ascension is different from others in four important respects:

1. Acts has the ascension occur neither in Jerusalem (present Marcan ending) nor in Bethany (Luke), but halfway between these two locations, on the Mount of Olives.

2. The time also is completely different, forty days after Easter when Mark and Luke have it occur.

3. The ascension is accentuated by a miracle as two presumably heavenly messengers are made to appear and participate in the event. "And while they (the disciples) were steadily looking into Heaven as he went, behold two men in white apparel stood by them" (Acts 1:10).

4. The fourth radical innovation in the Acts ascension account consists in remaking it into an announcement of Christ's second coming. "You men of Galilee, why do you stand looking into Heaven? This Jesus who was received up from you into Heaven shall so come in the same manner as you have beheld him going into Heaven" (Acts 1:11).

In light of Luke's usual record for high accuracy in his research, it is surprising that in Acts he should have strayed so far from the presumed truth at this point. Although one has come to expect elaboration in moving chronologically from book to book, it is remarkable to have one individual add so much to the progression of growth as in this instance. Furthermore, if Luke, as is generally supposed, wrote both his gospel and Acts, how could their descriptions of the ascension be so completely different. The most obvious answer is that some late irresponsible annotator must have inserted the ascension item into Acts 1.

Although Matthew does not make specific mention of an ascension, it would seem to be implied. However, according to that gospel writer the event would have occurred sometime after Easter at a fourth location, on a mountain in Galilee. "But the eleven disciples went into Galilee, to the mountain where Jesus had appointed them" (Matthew 28:16). Then followed his final commission to them (vss. 17-20), after which he presumably disappeared by ascending to Heaven.

The Gospel of John also records no actual ascension but clearly implies such. Jesus is represented as announcing his ascension early, in John 6:62: "What then if you should behold the Son of Man ascending where he was before?" John has Jesus announce it again to Mary Magdalene on Easter morning by saying "go to my brethren and say to them: 'I ascend to my Father and your Father, and my God and your God'" (John 20:17).

A comparison of the two "touching" passages in John are revealing. On Easter morning, Jesus is recorded as having said to Mary Magdalene, "Do not touch me, for I have not yet ascended to the Father" (John 20:17). By contrast, in the upper-room meeting one week later Jesus is quoted as having said to Thomas, "reach hither your hand and put it into my side" (John 20:27).

Two deductions follow. First, the conclusion seems necessitated that the author of the Fourth Gospel thought, with Luke and the expanded Mark, that the ascension occurred on Easter night. Second, and more important, contrast between the two "touching" statements indicates that John thought the second coming of Jesus had occurred one week after Easter, in the same upper room.

Expectation of a presumably remote second coming had become paired with the ascension in Acts 1:11. John, by contrast, made that expected event immediate. This second advent necessitated that it be paired with a second ascension at the end of chapter 21, also, like the first ascension in John, only implied but not specifically described. Consequently, John rates as the mathematical reporter, multiplying the Easter-evening gathering into three meetings with the disciples, with the minimal interval of a week between them. In the same way he multiplied the one ascension into two, perhaps considerably more than a week apart.

If Jesus had ascended to Heaven, the time and place probably would have been indelibly fixed in Christian memory. The difference in place of its supposed occurrence is perhaps the strongest evidence against the ascension's occurrence: from the upper room (Mark), from Bethany (Luke), from the Mount of Olives (Acts), from an appointed

mountain in Galilee (Matthew), and from the shores of the
Sea of Galilee (John).

The differences as to time of occurrence also are
significant. Mark's, Luke's and John's implied first
ascension took place on Easter night. Matthew's and John's
implied second ascension were staged at undesignated times
at remote locations in Galilee, evidently weeks later. Acts
states specifically that the ascension took place forty days
after Easter. All this adds up to a hodgepodge of
discrepancies and misinformation regarding a supposed
ascension that never occurred.

The concept of a second coming of Jesus made
Christianity competitive with Judaism. The final words of
the Old Testament tell how the prophet Elijah was expected
to return again to earth before the judgment day (Malachi
4:5 [3:23 in Hebrew]). Observant Jews still set a place for
Elijah at every Passover meal. At a certain point in the
seder someone goes to the door and opens it so Elijah can
come in if he should choose to stage his second coming by
descending from Heaven at the Passover and should chance to
arrive at that particular home. To compete with this Jewish
expectation of Elijah's second coming, it was rather
inevitable that Christianity would develop the correlative
belief in Jesus' second advent.

The claim that certain Old Testament leaders, and
people of other religions, have ascended to Heaven is built
on the theory of the universe which prevailed in those
days. The entire Bible is built on the pre-Copernican
assumption that we live on a flat earth. Over this is a
solid inverted bowl called the firmament. Above this vault
is a Heaven of delights, including golden streets,
fabulously high-rising apartments, exotic city parks, golden
harps, God's throne, etc. This material overworld was
regarded as only a short distance above earth, as witnessed
by the Babel people who thought they could build their tower
to Heaven (Genesis 11:4). Jacob's ladder reached from earth
to Heaven, with angels ascending and descending on it
(Genesis 28:12).

Advent of the Copernican cosmology (A.D. 1473-1543)
removed the Heaven above, with easy access to it.
Consequently, accounts of the ascension of biblical and
other religious leaders no longer ring true.

This has been a long story of growth from a Jesus who
probably finally died immediately after Easter, and whose
bones may even survive in their ossuary in Jerusalem today,
to the belief that he did not die again but ascended to
Heaven. This item of faith was then proliferated in
fivefold manner by the authors of the gospels and Acts,

eventuating ultimately with the derivative belief in the second coming. This was quite a superstructure to erect on the simple occurrence of Jesus' presumed death and burial.

Belief in the ascension served as a theological lifesaver for an Early Church that could not acknowledge the bodily remains of its deified founder. But it has landed the Church in the onus of having concocted one of the greatest falsehoods of the ages, one which is staged unabashed in most churches each Easter.

IV.

Easter Growth in New Testament Apocryphal Gospels

There exists what might well be called a counter-New
Testament. The accepted name for this body of writings is
the Apocryphal New Testament.[10] As the Old Testament
Apocrypha contains books not regarded as divinely inspired,
and therefore excluded from the Hebrew canon of Scripture,
the Apocryphal New Testament is made up of those early
Christian writings that were regarded as not authentic or
whose authority was questioned.

This material, which did not get into the Christian
canon, is a voluminous literature, much larger than the New
Testament itself. While in the New Testament the passion
and Easter are dealt with only two or three chapters at the
end of each gospel, in the Apocryphal New Testament whole
gospels are devoted to the events of those days. Notable
are the Gospels of Peter, Nicodemus, and Bartholomew. That
literature also includes the Book of the Resurrection of
Christ by Bartholomew the Apostle and the Book of John the
Evangelist. In addition, there are many Coptic, Syriac,
Greek, and Latin treatises that are hardly large enough to
be called gospels, plus many fragments and letters.

Although there is great variation in degree of
authenticity among these apocryphal materials, one can make

certain generalizations. What value there is in the
apocryphal gospels consists largely in what they have
appropriated in one way or another from the canonical
gospels. Careful study indicates that the apocryphal
writers have added little of an authentic nature. Most of
the content veers so far from the truth and is so flighty
that this body of literature has been called "the New
Testament gone wild."

Nevertheless, it must not be assumed that just because
an account is in the Apocrypha it is false and when in the
New Testament it is true. The three previous chapters have
shown that the apocryphal movement already had gained
unbelievable headway in the New Testament itself, to the
point that a startlingly high percent of the Easter story
consists of baseless apocryphal proliferations.

It seems wise that attention should be turned now to
these noncanonical gospels. Consideration will not be given
here to the portions of that writing which rehearse
authentic parts of the New Testament. Rather, the objective
will be to see how the apocryphal movement, already so
strong within the New Testament itself, became further
accentuated in the Apocryphal New Testament.

Although the order of events is frequently scrambled,
an attempt will be made here to consider them in proper
chronological sequence. With little by way of comment, this

literature will be allowed to speak for itself.

Attention may well be directed first to The Book of the Resurrection of Christ by Bartholomew the Apostle. He was a nondescript disciple, never mentioned in the New Testament except in routine lists of the disciples. In that gospel, whether by Bartholomew or an impostor writing in his name, the author claims to have been an eyewitness of all which he describes.

With Death and his six sons portrayed as supernatural beings, Bartholomew's Easter drama begins as these seven approach the tomb which contains Jesus' body. Death is in the lead. "He came to the tomb of Jesus with his six sons in the form of serpents. Jesus lay there . . . with his face and head covered with napkins. Death addressed his son the Pestilence, and described the commotion which had taken place in his domain. Then he spoke to the body of Jesus and asked, 'Who art thou?' Jesus removed the napkin that was on his face and looked in the face of Death and laughed at him. Death and his sons fled. Then they approached again, and the same thing happened. He addressed Jesus again at some length, suspecting, but not certain, who he was. Then Jesus rose and mounted into the chariot of the Cherubim."[11]

The Report of Pilate, concerning the events of those days, says that the resurrection took place at the third hour of the night, i.e., 9 p.m. At that time of year the

Jewish "first day of the week" began at approximately 6
p.m., on what we call Saturday evening. "On the first day
of the week, at the third hour of night, there was a great
light: the sun shone with unwonted brightness, men in
shining garments appeared in the air and cried out to the
souls in Hades to come up, and proclaimed the resurrection
of Jesus. The light continued all night. Many Jews
disappeared in the chasms which the earthquake had caused:
and all the synagogues except one fell down."[12]

In the supposed Story of Joseph of Arimathaea he is
made to say "The Jews imprisoned me on the evening of the
Sabbath" (Friday evening) because he had granted his
sepulchre for Jesus' entombment. Joseph then goes on to
tell that at 11:00 p.m. on Saturday evening (the 5th hour),
two hours after the 9:00 p.m. resurrection (at the 3rd
hour), Jesus came and rescued him by causing the entire
prison building to rise from off him. "When it was evening
on the first day of the week, at the fifth hour of the
night, Jesus came to me with the thief on the right hand.
There was a great light; the house was raised up by the four
corners and I went forth."[13]

Philogenes, owner of the garden in which Jesus was
entombed, told what he saw on the night of resurrection.
"At midnight he rose and went out and found all the orders
of angels: Cherubim, Seraphim, Powers, and Virgins. Heaven

opened, and the Father raised Jesus. Peter, too, was there
and supported Philogenes, or he would have died. The Savior
then appeared to them on the chariot of the Father . . . .
Believe me, my brethren the holy apostles, I, Bartholomew,
beheld the Son of God on the chariot of the Cherubim. All
the heavenly hosts were about him."[14]

In the Gospel of Bartholomew IV:1-13 that disciple
portrays himself as leader of the apostles. He describes a
conference with the risen Jesus on the Mount of Olives. "1
And he took them and brought them again unto the Mount of
Olives . . . . 7 When Jesus appeared again, Bartholomew said
unto him: Lord, show us the adversary of men that we may
behold him . . . .8 But Jesus looked upon him and said:
Thou bold heart! Thou askest for that which thou art not
able to look upon. 9 But Bartholomew was troubled and fell
at Jesus' feet and began to speak thus: . . . remember not
evil against me but grant me the word of mine asking
. . . .10 And as he thus spoke, Jesus raised him up and said
unto him: Bartholomew, wilt thou see the adversary of men?
I tell thee that when thou beholdest him, not thou only but
the rest of the apostles and Mary will fall on your faces
and become as dead corpses. 11 But they all said unto him:
Lord, let us behold him. 12 And he led them down from the
Mount of Olives and looked wrathfully upon the angels that
keep hell (Tartarus), and beckoned unto Michael to sound the

trumpet in the height of the heavens. And Michael sounded,
and the earth shook, and Beliar came up, being held by 660
(560 Gk., 6,064 Lat. 1, 6,060 Lat. 2) angels and bound with
fiery chains. 13 And the length of him was 1,600 cubits and
his breadth 40 (Lat. 1, 300; Slav. 17) cubits (Lat. 2, his
length 1,900 cubits, his breadth 700, one wing of him 80),
and his face was like a lightning of fire and his eyes full
of darkness (like sparks, Slav.). And out of his nostrils
came a stinking smoke; and his mouth was as the gulf of a
precipice, and the one of his wings was four-score
cubits."[15] The figure of 1,600 cubits would give Satan a
height of approximately 2,660 feet and the 80 cubits would
make each wing approximately 133 feet in length.

"14 And straightaway when the apostles saw him, they
fell to the earth on their faces and became as dead. 15 But
Jesus came near and raised the apostles and gave them a
spirit of power, and he saith unto Bartholomew: . . . Draw
near. And as Bartholomew drew near, fire was kindled on
every side, so that his garments appeared fiery. Jesus
saith to Bartholomew: As I said unto thee, tread upon his
neck and ask him what is his power. And Bartholomew went
and trode upon his neck, and pressed down his face into the
earth as far as his ears. 23 And Bartholomew saith unto
him; Tell me who thou art and what is thy name. And he said
to him: Lighten me a little, and I will tell thee who I am

and how I came hither, and what my work is and what my power
is. 24 And he lightened him and saith to him: Say all that
thou hast done and all that thou doest." Then follow
thirty-five verses in which Satan recounts his history. "60
Then Bartholomew commanded him to go into hell."[16]

The Story of Joseph of Arimathea asserts that the
resurrected Jesus, the liberated Joseph of Arimathaea, and
the repentant thief set out for Galilee as a trio: "and I
perceived Jesus first, and then the thief bringing a letter
to him, and as we journeyed to Galilee there was a very
great light, and a sweet fragrance came from the thief
. . . . When we saw the mark of the nails on the robber that
was crucified with thee and the light of the letters of thy
Godhead, the fire was quenched, being unable to bear the
light of the mark, and we were in great fear and crouched
down."[17]

The miraculous appearance of the repentant thief on
this trip is also described. "For we beheld the spotless
cross, with the robber flashing with light and shining with
seven times the light of the sun, and trembling came on us,
when we heard tne crashing of them beneath the earth, and
with a great voice the ministers of Hades said with us:
Holy, Holy, Holy, is he that was in the highest in the
beginning: and the powers sent up a cry, saying, Lord, thou
hast been manifested in heaven and upon earth, giving joy

unto the worlds (ages) and saving thine own creation from
death. V. 1 And as I went with Jesus and the robber to
Galilee, the form of Jesus was changed and he became wholly
light, and angels ministered to him and he conversed with
them."[17]

The disciple John then is said to have appeared and
spoke to Jesus, asking who was accompanying him in such
great pomp. Jesus said that this was the repentant thief
who, in reward for his repentance, would enjoy Paradise as
"his alone until the great day come . . . . Then suddenly
the thief appeared and John fell to the earth: for he was
now like a king in great might, clad with the cross. And
the voice of a multitude was heard: Thou art come into the
place of paradise prepared for thee: we are appointed to
serve thee by him that sent thee until the great day."[18]
The "we" here probably refers to the hosts of heavenly
angels who were commanded to serve the repentant thief until
the judgment day.

After arriving in Galilee Jesus gathered the disciples
and delivered to them a postresurrection "sermon on the
mount." "1 And he departed with them unto the mount Mauria
(Lat. 2, Mambre), and sat in the midst of them. 2 But they
doubted to question him, being afraid. 3 And Jesus answered
and said unto them: Ask me what ye will that I should teach
you, and I will show it to you. For yet seven days, and I

ascend unto my Father, and I shall no more be seen of you in
this likeness. 4 But they, yet doubting, said unto him:
Lord, show us the deep (abyss) according unto thy promise.
5 And Jesus said unto them: It is not good (Lat. 2, is
good) for you to see the deep: notwithstanding if ye desire
it, according to my promise, come, follow me and behold. 6
And he led them away into a place that is called Cherubim
(Cherukt Slav., Chairoudec Gr., Lat. 2 omits), that is the
place of truth. 7 And he beckoned unto the angels of the
West, and the earth was rolled up like a volume of a book
and the deep was revealed unto them. 8 And when the
apostles saw it, they fell on their faces upon the earth. 9
But Jesus raised them up, saying: Said I not unto you, 'It
is not good for you to see the deep'. And again he beckoned
unto the angels, and the deep was covered up."[19]

"The Father sent the Son down into Galilee to console
the apostles and Mary: and he came and blessed them and
showed them his wounds, and committed them to the care of
Peter, and gave them their commission to preach. They
kissed his side and sealed themselves with the blood that
flowed thence. He went up to heaven."[20]

Thomas' son Siophanes died and Thomas did not arrive
until the seventh day after the death. "He went to the tomb
and raised him in the name of Jesus. Siophanes told him of
the taking of his soul by Michael: how it sprang from his

body and lighted on the hand of Michael, who wrapped it in a
fine linen cloth: how he crossed the river of fire . . .
how in heaven he saw the twelve splendid thrones of the
apostles, and was not permitted to sit on his father's
throne . . . . He, Siophanes, addressed the people and told
his story: and Thomas baptized 12,000 of them, . . . Then
Thomas mounted on a cloud and it took him to the Mount of
Olives and to the apostles, . . ."[21] This shows how even
doubting Thomas became independent of distance by being
carried about on clouds.

The Book of the Resurrection of Christ by Bartholomew
The Apostle goes on to describe a "last supper" of the
disciples with Jesus after his resurrection. It records an
in excelsis celebration of the eucharist in a manner
outdoing even the most advanced transubstantiation theory.
"His Body was on the Table about which they were assembled;
and they divided it. They saw the blood of Jesus pouring
out as living blood down into the cup. Peter said: God
hath loved us more than all, in letting us see these great
honours: and our Lord Jesus Christ hath allowed us to
behold and hath revealed to us the glory of his body and his
divine blood. They partook of the body and blood -- and
then they separated and preached the word."[22]

The Apostle then goes on to describe the ascension and
Jesus' arrival in Heaven, accompanied by all the hosts he

had redeemed from Hell. "Jesus and the redeemed souls
ascended into Heaven, and the Father crowned him. The glory
of this scene Bartholomew could not describe . . . . Then
follows a series of hymns sung in heaven, eight in all,
which accompany the reception of Adam and the other holy
souls into glory. Adam was eighty cubits high and Eve
fifty. They were brought to the Father by Michael.
Bartholomew had never seen anything to compare with the
beauty and glory of Adam, save that of Jesus. Adam was forgiven, and all the angels and saints rejoiced and saluted
him, and departed each to their place. Adam was set at the
gate of life to greet all the righteous as they enter, and
Eve was set over all the women who had done the will of God,
to greet them as they come into the city of Christ. As for
me, Bartholomew, I remained many days without food or drink,
nourished by the glory of the vision."[23] The 80 cubits
for Adam would have made him approximately 120 feet tall,
and the fifty for Eve, approximately 75 feet tall. So, in
the Apocrypha, our first parents were people of physical
stature.

While only Jesus is recorded as having ascended to
Heaven in the New Testament, Bartholomew states that all the
disciples were carried up with Jesus. Most vivid is the
description of how Jesus took the apostles with him from
presumably the first Heaven into the seventh Heaven. "The
heavens were opened and we all went up into the seventh

heaven . . . He prayed the Father to bless us. The Father,
with the Son and the Holy Ghost, laid His hand on the head
of Peter (and made him archbishop of the whole world: Paris
B). . . . none who is not ordained by him shall be
accepted. Each of the apostles was separately blessed . . .
The apostles kissed and blessed him. And then, with Mary,
they offered the Eucharist."[24]

   In looking back over this sampling of materials from
the Apocryphal New Testament, it is apparent that they
reflect ever-mounting cycles of oral tradition that seem to
have arisen by spontaneous generation. The worst that can
be said for those authors is that they were fabricators who
chronicled items which have no basis in fact. The kindest
words that may be offered in their defense is that they were
gifted with extremely fertile imaginations. At least, these
citations from the apocryphal gospels witness to an amazing
departure from truth.

V.

Continuing Ministry of Jesus in Other Parts of the World

The collection known as the Apocryphal New Testament contains only a small portion of the apocryphal stories that have arisen concerning Jesus' Easter and subsequent experiences. A favorite form of medieval and modern apocrypha assumes that, instead of dying immediately after Easter or ascending to Heaven, Jesus slipped away unnoticed from Palestine following that night and journeyed to other lands where he carried on further ministries. There are accounts of purported work by him in such countries as Persia, India, China, the Balkans, France, the British Isles, North America, and even Central America with its lore about "the great white father." By way of sampling, attention here will be devoted to only two of these areas.

1. Jesus, Mary Magdalene, and Children go to France

A very old but very new theory asserts that Jesus went into Central Europe following Easter. This view has been revived today by three English journalists[25] and they have been refuted with equal vigor by two specialists in medieval history.[26]

This most intimate of the reported post-Easter experiences claims that Jesus married Mary Magdalene and had a
family of children by her. The wedding at Cana of Galilee,
described in the second chapter of John's gospel, is
regarded in this view as Jesus' own wedding at which he
unveiled his miraculous powers by turning six storage jars
of water into wine. Her sister and brother were Martha and
Lazarus. This brother, who later was raised from the dead
by Jesus, is credited with having written most of the Fourth
Gospel. Since it is assumed that all rabbis were married in
Jesus' day, that Jesus was called Rabbi six times in the
Fourth Gospel is taken as proof that he was married.

Either Jesus or his disciples staged the affair on
Calvary and by subterfuge he escaped his supposed
crucifixion. According to the favorite view, Simon of
Cyrene was crucified instead. Jesus was not the type of
person who would have abandoned his religious career so
prematurely.

At the time of the Good Friday-Easter crisis Jesus and
his family supposedly slipped out of Palestine unnoticed and
moved into Central Europe where they finally settled in
southeastern France. The family was accompanied by Lazarus
and Joseph of Arimathea. Mary Magdalene is supposed to have
taken choice Christian relics with her, such as pieces of
the alabaster cruse that contained the ointment with which
she anointed the feet of Jesus, the pair of sandals which

she removed from his feet on that notable occasion, and
especially the Holy Grail, the magic cup from which Jesus
and his disciples drank at the Last Supper.

Discovery of sculptures and stone cuttings of Mary as a
favorite art theme in the region of Rennes, France, has led
to the conclusion that the family settled in that region.
It is assumed that Mary spent her final years in a hermitage
or cave in that locality.

Since there is no evidence of an extended ministry of
Jesus in those parts, it is assumed that he did not spend
full time with the family but returned to Palestine and was
thought probably to have died, at the age of eighty, during
the siege of Masada in A.D. 73.

The descendants of Jesus and Mary in their region of
Central Europe became a superior race called the
Merovingians. That name was thought to have been derived
from Mary and is the prime evidence that the holy family
settled in those parts. These Merovingians were different
from all other governmental groups in Europe in that they
had Jesus' divine blood, through Mary Magdalene, coursing
through their veins. Reinforced by this unique asset, these
Merovingians became the leading dynasty in Central Europe
which they dominated from A.D. 500 until 751.

This Merovingian theory rests primarily on a false
etymological derivation, juggling biblical facts to fit into
the desired story, combined with baseless suppositions.

2. The Ahmadiyya Story of Christ in India

Another family of traditions assumes that Jesus journeyed eastward, rather than northwestward, deep into the Orient. A synopsis may be given here of the view that Jesus journeyed to India, spent the remainder of his life in that part of the world, and eventually died there. The claims for such a journey and terminal mission in Jesus' life have been summarized by the present-day Ahmadiyya Muslim, Sufi Bengalee.[27]

It is not stated whether Jesus slipped away in secret or departed from Jerusalem openly for India. On two occasions Jesus said he had been sent to "the lost sheep of the house of Israel" (Matthew 10:6; 15:24). "Out of the twelve tribes of Israel, only two were in the country where Jesus taught his Gospels and was crucified. In order to fulfill his mission, Jesus must, of necessity, go to that country which was inhabited by the remaining tribes of Israel . . . Hence, we must admit that either Jesus Christ did not fulfill his mission or he went to that part of the world where were the remaining ten tribes of Israel who undoubtedly were the overwhelming majority. Historical investigations reveal to us that the people of Kashmir, India, Afghanistan, and the surrounding provinces represent the ten lost tribes of Israel."[28]

A historical work <u>Rawzatus-Safaa</u> tells of an encounter
on the way to India with the authorities at the city of
Nisibis in north Syria, near the present Iraqi border.
"In that trip, he was accompanied by some of his disciples
whom he sent into the city to preach. False and unbecoming
rumors had, however, been prevalent in the city about Jesus
and his mother, on account of which the Governor of the city
had the disciples arrested and summoned Jesus. Jesus
miraculously healed some people and performed other
wonders. The result was that the ruler of that territory
with all his armies and people became the follower of
Jesus." This "helps us to trace the route he followed in
his long journey. He came to India by way of Persia and
Afghanistan, halting at Nasibain or Nasibus on his way."[29]

"Jesus . . . went to India and paid a visit to Tibet
where he delivered his great message to the Buddhists of
that country, who readily accepted him as the <u>Messian</u>, as he
fully answered the description of the prophecy prevailing
among them."[30] "In one version of the story he is said to
have come to confer and argue with the Buddhist monks on the
doctrine of reincarnation . . . "[31]

The many similarities which are found between the
teachings of Jesus and Buddhist teachings are therefore
explained, by those who claim he was in India, through
Christ's transformation of Buddhism while he was in those

parts. "The following circumstances specifically identify
Jesus to have been the fulfillment of Buddha's prophecy
about the advent of the Messiah. First: The prophecy
states that five hundred years after the time of Buddha when
the religion would be in a state of decay, the new Buddha
Messiah would appear in order to restore the religion to its
pristine purity. No one needs to be told that Jesus came
precisely five centuries after Buddha. Second: According
to Buddha's prophecy, the would be Buddha, the Messiah would
be 'Bagwa' -- light in complexion. It is a well-known fact
that Gautama Buddha who was born in India five hundred years
before the Christian era, was of dark complexion. And Jesus
Christ coming as ne did from Palestine was comparatively of
much lighter complexion. Hence, the Buddha Messiah could
have been none other than Jesus Christ."[32]

"In short, Jesus came to the Punjab by way of
Afghanistan and after paying visits to Benares, Nepal and
Tibet, finally arrived in Kashmir where he settled. The
discovery of the tomb with the inscription 'Yus Asaf'
decisively settles the question. There is a tradition among
the people of Kashmir that the tomb belongs to one Yus Asaf
-- who was a Nabi (Prophet), . . . He came there some 1900
years ago from some western country." Jesus "at last
reached Kashmir, and there he died. A historical work, the
Tarikhi Azami, written some two hundred years ago, says

regarding this tomb: 'The tomb is generally known as that
of a prophet. He was a prince who came from a foreign
land. He was perfect in piety, righteousness and devotion.
He was made a prophet by God and was engaged in preaching to
the people of Cashmere. His name was Yus Asaf.'"[33]

"The following circumstances prove that Yus Asaf could
be none other than Jesus. 1. The word 'Yus' is no other
than Yasu, the Arabic name for Jesus. Asaf is the Hebrew
form of Asaph, the gatherer, so it comes to mean, 'Jesus the
gatherer,' as Jesus came to gather the lost tribes of
Israel. 2. He is known as Nabi, a prophet among the
Moslems. The word 'nabi' occurs only in two languages,
Arabic and Hebrew. He could not be a Moslem as none other
than the Holy Prophet has been called 'Nabi'; so he must be
a Hebrew prophet. 3. It is noteworthy that there exists a
striking resemblance between the teachings of Yus Asaf and
those of Jesus."[34]

Sufi Bengalee's booklet has a picture of the tomb,[35]
but no measurements are given. From the fence-height in the
picture one would guess that it is an estimated forty-eight
by seventy-two feet, and twenty feet high to the bottom of
the roof. The three-tiered roof, in pyramidal form, mounts
to another probably twenty feet in height. Along the front
are five Roman arches, at least twelve feet high, and three
much wider ones along the side. If the inside is comparable
to the outside, it is a most luxurious tomb.

An unusual amount of attention has been given to this seemingly convincing case for Jesus having been in India. Those assertions have been presented as an illustration of the best of the many stories, ostensibly carefully documented, tnat have placed post-resurrection years of Jesus in many parts of the world.

It is regrettable that space cannot be taken to offer an item by item examination of these Indian claims. It must suffice to give attention to only three matters. (1) That Yus Asaf is the same as Jesus is a very dubious etymology. It reminds one of the Anglo-Israel Society's claim that Anglo-Saxon is a derivative from Isaac's Son, upon which that society bases its claim that the English people are the ten lost tribes of Israel. (2) The ten lost tribes are presumably not to be found in India, England, America or any other remote region but rather in areas nearer to Palestine. Tney presumably have become blended into the populations of Syria, Iraq, and Iran, and are a substantial part of the people called Arabs. (3) Tradition says Yus Asaf was a wealthy prince, and the luxury of his tomb attests to that claim. That such a structure should have been the tomb of a humble Jesus, who did not own even two suits of clothes, seems extremely unlikely.

3. Endless Proliferations on Post-Easter World Ministries

Lines of investigation, such as just offered in sections 1 and 2 concerning a lifetime of post-Easter ministry in France or India, show that the claims for such extended public work do not hold up under critical examination. The same may be said for the multitudes of other legends recording supposed ministries of Jesus to peoples in other parts of the world.[36] Such ostensible records presumably are but extrabiblical extensions of the apocryphal movement. Whether in the canonical gospels, in the Apocryphal New Testament, or in the still later legends of Jesus that have sprung up over all the world, these myriads of baseless stories that have proliferated themselves make it almost impossible to retract attention to the attested events of Easter and the days immediately following.

VI.

Easter Overshadowed by Pentecost and Passion Observances

In retrospect, it was seen that the events of Easter day made little impression on the supposed Holy City. Residents of Jerusalem were in sadness because the authorities had crucified the one who, they hoped, would liberate their country from Roman rule and set himself up as a triumphant king. The disciples were depressed because they had lost hope of gaining the cabinet positions which they had expected. The whole company of Jesus' followers were disillusioned, bewildered, and incredulous as to what had happened. Since they regarded Jesus' coming to them in the upper room on Easter evening as but a phantom appearance, it did not lift them from their despair over having lost their leader. Apparently, most of the disciples left for Galilee at once to resume their former vocations.

If there had been only Easter, the Christian Church might never have come into existence. As recorded in Acts 2, this development did not take place until five weeks after Easter when a thunderstorm with its "mighty wind" came suddenly, and lightning struck the building in which Jesus' followers were meeting. "Tongues of fire" engulfed the congregation. In an age when every shaft of lightning continued to be construed as an act of God for some specific purpose, tnis fiery conflagration was regarded as God's bestowing his Holy Spirit upon the assembled group. The tnree thousand who were converted in consequence of that event contrasted dramatically with the disillusionment on Easter and its impotence to bring about any transformation.

From New Testament days to the present, Easter has been marred by its association with the gruesome elements that have attached themselves to supposed Holy Week observances. There is something paranoic about the passion celebrations. It is as if a widow were to re-enact the death of her belated husband each year on the anniversary of his demise. She would retrace the steps in his illness which led up to the fatal moment. She would have the funeral service re-enacted in paying her dutiful tributes eacn year to the one she had loved. It might be asked, "What would such a cycle of annual commemorations do to tne bereaved widow?"

Uncanny though it may be, this is what the Church has been doing for nineteen centuries. By encouraging worshipers to follow the stations of the cross weekly, or even daily, liturgical churches have caused Easter to be overshadowed by the agonies associated with Calvary. The ultimate travesty is the annual funeral procession from the judgment hall, up the Via Dolorosa, to Golgotha, stopping along the way at the original stations of the cross for a brief service at each. The three-hour vigil of Jesus' last words from the cross on each Good Friday in many churches is another dubious practice. Little wonder that supposed Holy Week became an open season on Christ killers in Eastern Europe when Jews cowered in fear and had to remain indoors during that week lest they be killed. The numerous passion plays in Eastern European countries became one of the most deleterious practices in any religion, relighting the fires of anti-Semitism at each performance.

Easter also has suffered through being overpowered by passion symbolisms. The sadistic picture of Jesus' bleeding heart has become an essential home decoration in major portions of Christendom. The crucifix, with bleeding hands, side, and feet, has been normative in churches through the ages. In reaction against this representation, Protestants have removed the victim but have retained the empty cross. It seems strange that passion mania dominated the Church to the point of enthroning as Christianity's symbol the cross of terror and suffering rather than any emblem from Jesus' ministry or Easter.

In light of all these detrimental effects of Holy-Week observances throughout the centuries, it might be wished that different types of celebrations had replaced them. Instead of dwelling on the morbidity of trial, cross, body, blood, and the eeriness connected with the tomb, dramatizations from the life and teachings of Jesus would seem to have been more fitting.

Easter was also bypassed in the evolution of Christianity's most sacred rite, the re-enactment of Maundy Thursday evening. The Lord's Supper of the apostolic age was a memorial service bringing remembrance of Jesus' life and teachings, a sacrament of common union and fellowship between believers and between them and the immortal Christ. In the course of time this rite became diminished into tokens of bread and wine, foreshadowing the crucifixion. This Eucharist or Communion increasingly became elevated as the chief rite of the Church. Accelerating observance of this ritual daily, weekly, monthly or even quarterly, left Easter in comparative oblivion, to be observed on only one day each year.

Most branches of the Church have come to focus on the body and blood, far from the Easter emphasis. By the claim of transubstantiation the bread and wine are changed into the actual body and blood of Christ as the Catholic priest offers up the elements. Even though the bread remains bread and the wine remains wine, by consubstantiation the Lutheran minister's prayer is thought to cause the actual body and blood of Christ to become present with the bread and wine. Except among denominations of the Zwinglian Reformation, where remembrance remains uppermost, the ministers of other mainline Protestant denominations increasingly are presenting Communion as symbolically "tne body of Christ" and "the blood of Christ." All this stress on eating the body and drinking the blood, whether actually or only symbolically, would probably cause a visitor from Mars to say that Christianity is a cannibal religion, at wnose most sacred rite worshippers eat the flesh and drink the blood of their founder.

The chief sacrament of the Church might well have been built around the Beatitudes as a more worthy replacement. Such a sacrament would have given to Jesus' eight Beatitudes the prestige they deserve as the fullest expression of his distinctive religion, always reminding congregants of the life that he expects from his followers.

As to the Easter celebration itself, the Church might well consider itself at a parting of the ways. Four possibilities for celebration would seem possible.

1. The Church may, and probably will, continue Easter observance as in the past. This means that, since they are more spectacular and miraculous, the Easter stories as found in Matthew and John will continue to be read in churches on Easter day. In so doing the Church becomes guilty of disseminating from her pulpits on tnat most sacred day of the church year a profusion of falsehoods. In light of our better understandings of the Bible, it is an unforgivable

travesty for that great day, to be given over to the further perpetuation of untruths.

2. Taking advantage of discerning biblical studies, the tragedy of what has happened by way of unpardonable expansion of the Easter story even in the Bible might be explained. Pursuant thereto, the Scripture readings on Easter might well be confined to what is found in Mark and Luke. In so doing, the pulpit would be portraying the true picture of Easter, showing how the followers of Jesus were frightened, incredulous, and not believing that what they saw was Jesus, but only a terrifying ghost with whom they refused to make physical contact or even speak. This admittedly is a very uninspiring picture of Easter, an instance where the truth is very bitter. It is hardly possible that Christianity could be satisfied with such an uninviting portrayal.

3. Another way out would be to ignore Easter and blot it out of the church year, the option chosen by most New Testament writers. Possibly they deserve credit for keener discernment in avoiding mention of Easter. Could it be that they did not want to defame the disciples further by rehearsing their disgraceful actions on that day of days when Jesus returned to them that evening in the upper room? Perhaps, realizing that most of the Easter story was a quagmire of falsehood, those authors wanted nothing to do

with it. Possibly Paul and Peter in their letters, writers
of the other epistles, and the author of Revelation were
wise in having a Christianity with no Easter day. This
blackout has left 22 of the New Testament's 27 books and 251
of its 257 chapters with no mention of Easter.

4. Since the accounts of Easter have been seen to be
so honeycombed with false accretions, belief in ghosts, and
the indolence of incredulous disciples, one might wish that
a new approach to Easter celebration might evolve, even
after these nineteen centuries. Instead of repeating
uncritically and perpetuating further the profuse falsehoods
of the Easter chapters each spring, it would be fortunate if
that day might develop into a great annual feast of
renewal. Such a festival of redevotion might consist in
enthroning anew the immortal Sermon on the Mount with its
high demand for righteous living. This observance would be
a feast of life worthy of the Jesus who, "seeing the
multitudes went up into the mountain and, when he had sat
down, his disciples came unto him and he opened his mouth
and taught them" (Matthew 5:1-2).

Such annual glorification of the Sermon on the Mount
would be devoted to the main purpose of religion, to add a
spiritual dimension for the purpose of transforming our
lives into a world fellowship of spiritual beings. This
type of celebration might adopt as the symbol of

Christianity the living Jesus, of the Sermon on the Mount
and Easter, rather than a dead crucifix or an empty cross.

Easter is too precious a day to lose, but it is too
sacred a day to have it continue to be prostituted into
being the crown of the supposed Christian year with respect
to dispensing falsehoods.

VII.

Valediction on the Miracle of Easter Growth

This retracing of the Easter story has been an amazing odyssey of discovery. It has been a long journey from the relatively small nucleus of truth to the almost endless fictional proliferations. How this Easter story grew, from gospel to gospel and beyond, might have been called "From Molenill to Mountain" or even "From Anthill to Complex of Mountain Ranges."

Now that the story is ended, and the dizzying heights of exegetical fancy have been scaled, from these Mount Everest summits it can be a source of satisfaction to look back over the upward trail which has been followed. This remarkable fictional ascent began from the plains of truth, as described in Part I, with their short, modest, and valid account of the Easter occurrences.

Part II has shown how, even within the canonical New Testament, the later gospel writers (Matthew and John) allowed themselves to be carried away with the popular escalation of the assertions regarding what took place on that day. Spurred on by new and spurious emergent tneologies, the Easter story became so pyramided and inflated as to become almost unrecognizable. Easter facts became heightened into a galaxy of miracles and fanciful

reconstructions. Under this avalanche of later and more
spectacular easterisms, the sober record of what happened on
that significant day has become obscured and largely lost,
even within the New Testament itself.

The second stage in this drama of growth consisted in
the irresponsible and reckless embroidering of biblical
facts by the new breed of supposedly Christian writers who
produced what have come to be called the apocryphal
gospels. These contain traditions that had gone wild.
Those writers must subconsciously have felt that the more
falsehoods that could be piled on the Easter story, the
better. At least, it can be said that those impostors,
usually masquerading as among the twelve original disciples,
had extremely fertile imaginations. The main tragedy of the
apocryphal movement consisted in the way so many of its
fancies became woven into the theologies of the Medieval
Church.

Supreme credit should go to certain leading third-
century and fourth-century church leaders who became alarmed
over what was happening. Since they saw the danger that
Christianity was about to become but a bundle of theological
lies, they sought to prevent those incoming floods of
falsity from making further inroads into Christian
literature.

Those bishops accomplished this security measure by forming a canon of New Testament materials, books that were deemed sufficiently acceptable for use in worship and instruction. With certain marginal disagreements, twenty-seven books finally weathered the scrutiny of leading diocesan authorities to form what we call the canonical New Testament. Its purpose was to prevent further apocryphal intrusions into the mainstream of Christian thought. Although the bishops apparently despaired of weeding out the apocryphal portions from the newly canonized gospels, those religious leaders at least prevented their sacred literature from becoming a quagmire of falsity.

If religion is to have a foundation of truth, the Easter story is a good place to begin by treasuring the apparently valid records mediated to us by Mark and Luke. Jesus spoke of one house built on a rock foundation and another on the sand. It would seem, if the Church is to survive, that it should be built upon the rock foundation of truth rather than the shifting sands or fanciful elabora- tions and theological inventions. By making a separation between the genuine and spurious records, as has been done in this present study, it is hoped that Christianity may become a religion built more upon truth and less on pious fictions.

Notes   Part III

1. R.H. Charles, _Apocrypha_ and _Pseudepigrapha_, Vol. 2, _Pseudepigrapha_, Oxford, Clarendon Press, 1913, _Enoch_, pp. 163-281 and _The Book of the Secrets of Enoch_, pp. 425-469.

2. _Enoch_, 70:1-2.

3. James Pritchard, _Ancient Near Eastern Texts_, Princeton, P. Univ. Press, 1956, p. 44.

4. Charles, _Pseudepigrapha_, pp. 407-424, especially section 2 on p. 407 and note 12 on p. 422.

5. Mark 9:2-13; Luke 9:28-36; Matthew 17:1-13.

6. _Ecclesiasticus_ 48:9.

7. _The Ascension of Isaiah_, chs. 7, 8, and 11.

8. James Hastings, ed., _Encyclopedia of Religion and Ethics_, Vol. 1, p. 152.

9. _ibid._, pp. 151-153.

10. Montague R. James, _The Apocryphal New Testament_. Oxford, Clarendon Press, 1924.

11. _ibid._, pp. 182-183.

12. _ibid._, p. 154.

13. _ibid._, p. 164.

14. _ibid._, pp. 183-184.

15. _ibid._, pp. 173-174.

16. _ibid._, pp. 174-175, 179.

Notes   Part III (cont'd.)

17. ibid., p. 164.

18. ibid., p. 165.

19. ibid., pp. 172-173.

20. ibid., p. 185.

21. ibid., p. 185.

22. Ibid., 185-186.

23. ibid., 184.

24. ibid., 184-185.

25. Richard Leigh, Henry Lincoln, and Mishael Baigent, Holy
     Grail, Holy Blood. Dell, paperback, 1983.

26. Patricia and Lionel Fanthorpe, The Holy Grail Revealed,
     North Hollywood, Newcastle Publ Co., 1982.

27. Sufi Mutiur Rahman Bengalee, The Tomb of Jesus, Qadain
     (India), The Nazir Dawato Tabligh, Ahmadiyya
     Community, 1963.

28. ibid., pp. 31-32.

29. ibid., pp. 35-37.

30. ibid., pp. 49-50

31. ibid., p. 40.

32. ibid., p. 51.

33. ibid., pp. 37-38.

34. ibid., p. 38.

Notes   Part III (cont'd.)

35. <u>ibid</u>., On the back of title page.

36. Selma Lagerlof, tr. by V.S. Howard, <u>Christ</u> <u>Legends</u>,
     N.Y., Henry Holt, 1908; A.S. Rappoport, <u>Medieval</u>
     <u>Legends</u> <u>of</u> <u>Christ</u>, N.Y., Scribners, 1935.

PART IV

GROWTH IN THE MARY STORIES

Eve and Mary vie with each other for position as the
most famous woman of all time. However, since Eve was only
the hypothetical first woman in existence and mother of all
humanity, Mary is left holding prestige as the best-known
historical woman in the nearer Orient and Western World. In
giving conception and birth to the most famous individual in
history, she was the beginning of the whole Christian
enterprise. Since Joseph is never mentioned in the Synoptic
Gospels after Jesus' twelfth year, it is assumed that he
died sometime thereafter, leaving Mary with support of the
Nazareth family. Next to Jesus himself, she rates as
perhaps the most important person in Christian history. Few
individuals have experienced such a wide range of fortune,
from obscurity to cosmic triumph.

In spite of her fame, it is embarrassing to discover
how few facts are available concerning Mary. Even more
amazing has been her fundamental change in attitude as she
has climbed the ladder of fortune. Although she has been
deluged with praise during the twenty centuries of Christian
history, it is surprising to find how little in the way of
discerning appraisal has been written about her.

The following study is an attempt to supply this need
by showing the steps by which the Mary figure has grown from

age to age, changing and mushrooming from a very human person to tne point of becoming regarded as an invincible supernatural being. This has been a long journey of achievement and it is our privilege to relive with her the adventures along the way.

The following pages are presented as a notable case study in how religious traditions develop.

I.

The Real Mary of the Synoptic Gospels

The purpose of this study is essentially to see how
Mary, the mother of Jesus, fared in respect to the events
associated with Easter day. However, it is rather
surprising to find that, according to the three Synoptic
Gospels of Matthew, Mark, and Luke, she was not present in
Jerusalem on that occasion. Therefore, to find the picture
of the real Mary, as of Easter day, it is necessary to
search the pre-Easter records.

The good relations between Joseph and Jesus, and
appreciation of the son's dreams and aspirations, is
indicated by Jesus' conceiving of God as the loving heavenly
Father. By contrast, in the Synoptic Gospels Jesus never
said any good word about his mother and she never said a
good word about him. She appears only twice in the gospel
record plus two references to her.

1. In the Temple at Twelve

Search for the real Mary begins with Jesus at the age
of twelve where we get the first inkling that the
relationships between him and his mother were already quite

strained. To understand that revealing episode, recorded
only in Luke 2:41-50, it is necessary to assume that Jesus
became enamored with the temple at this first contact with
it and immediately resolved to spend his coming years there
as an attendant to the priests. Inspired by his cousin
John's presumably being reared by the Essene priests at the
desert monastery of Qumran (Luke 1:80) and Samuel's living
with Priest Eli at the Shiloh sanctuary (I Samuel 1-3),
Jesus evidently expressed to his parents his determination
to remain at the temple.

However, the parents evidently forced Jesus to return
with them following the Passover. During their first
forenoon on the road Jesus likely mulled over his
disappointment. During that afternoon he evidently gained
courage to slip away unnoticed from the Nazareth group and
return to the temple where he was hospitably received by the
priests that evening.

The parents did not get back to the temple until the
third day, likely in the morning. They found him "sitting
in the midst of the doctors, both hearing them and asking
them questions." Instead of listening to the agility of her
son and hearing what was transpiring, Mary rudely
interrupted the interchange by scolding her son before his
admirers: "Why have you dealt thus with us?" Jesus must
have been mortified at being exposed in public. He replied,

"How is it that you searched for me? Didn't you know that I must be in my Father's house?" He was virtually saying, "I said I wanted to stay in the temple."

The parents apparently punctured his dream at once by forcing Jesus to return with them to Nazareth. There it was made certain that no such thing could occur again as he "was made subject to them" (Luke 2:51) and was denied attendance at future Passovers in Jerusalem.

It is worthy of observation that Joseph never said a word in this whole affair. He likely was sympathetic to Jesus' desires in the matter. This episode probably is of great importance in revealing an unsympathetic attitude of Mary toward her son, as early as in his twelfth year. Already he had grown ahead of his mother in spiritual matters while she could envision his future as only that of another carpenter.

2. Visit to Jesus' Preaching

After Jesus' ministry had come to receive notable public attention, some of his Nazareth boyhood friends went to hear him teach on an occasion when he was so surrounded by multitudes that neither he nor the disciples were able even to eat. "And the multitude came together again, so they could not so much as eat bread. And when his friends

heard it, they went out to lay hold on him, for they said,
'He is beside himself'" (Mark 3:20-21). These "friends,"
foiled in their purpose by the protective multitude,
returned to Nazareth and evidently informed Mary that her
son had become insane.

Shortly thereafter, an investigating committee on
un-Palestinian activities from the Jerusalem heirarchy came
to Galilee and made an investigation of Jesus' work. "And
the scribes who came down from Jerusalem said, 'He has
Beelzebul' and 'As the prince of demons he casts out
demons'" (Mark 3:22). When this official word came to the
Nazareth family, asserting that their son and brother had
become none other than an incarnation of the worst demon in
existence, Mary apparently was stunned, but not surprised.

Community pressure upon Mary must have been terrific to
bring this apostate son home and stop the disgrace he was
bringing upon her family and upon the fair name of the
Nazareth village. The mother, brothers, and sisters of
Jesus evidently believed all of the terrible charges that
were being brought against their son and brother. The
distraught family finally took action by deciding to bring
this errant member home and diminish the disgrace that was
overwhelming them. They found the house where he was
teaching but discovered that he was surrounded by an
inpenetrable multitude. "And his mother and his brothers

came and, standing on the outside, they sent to him, calling him. And a multitude was sitting about him. And they said to him, 'Behold your mother and your brothers without are seeking for you'" (Mark 3:31-32).

Jesus must have heard about the attitudes toward him which had come to prevail in Nazareth. Sensing that the family group had come in an antagonistic mood, with the purpose of bringing his ministry to an end and taking him home, Jesus refused to stop his teaching in order to confer with them. Even when they sent a message to him by word of mouth from person to person that they wanted to see him, he kept on teaching. He may well have thought it might not hurt them to hear a little of his utterances directly, rather than to trust in rumors.

As the attitudes of Mary and the brothers toward him did not change, and since the family group probably was anxious to return home, there is no indication that Jesus even spoke to them on that occasion. As the people in his audience must have been shocked by what seemed rudeness toward his mother and brothers, Jesus closed the matter by issuing a blistering broadside. "And he answered them and said, 'Who is my mother and my brothers?' And looking around on those who were round about him, he said, 'Behold my mother and my brothers! For whoever does the will of God, the same is my brother, and sister, and mother'" (Mark 3:33-35).

Jesus had grown away from his mother and brothers to the point that a great gulf existed between him and them, so they meant no more to him than other people. In fact, they meant far less than the people around him who were intent on "doing the will of God." By contrast, the implication is that his mother and brothers were not doing "the will of God." Since the ties of the spirit are far stronger than the ties of the flesh, he had turned from his mother and brothers to his spiritual mother, brothers, and sisters.

These biting words, plus not stopping his teaching to speak with family members, must have been taken by these Nazareth visitants as a cruel disowning of his family.

3. Visit Home to Nazareth

Later Jesus apparently repented of his rudeness to the family group on that occasion by refusing to speak with them and virtually disowning them. To make amends he evidently decided to interrupt his ministry by going home, in an attempt to bring about a reconciliation with his mother, his family, his relationship, and the citizens of Nazareth (Luke 4:16-30).

That mission failed tragically in its purpose. Even though neither Mary nor any other family member were named specifically, the account is full of inferences. It may be

guessed that Jesus' return brought only new turmoil into the
Nazareth home. The fact that no family members are
mentioned in connection with the synagogue episode may
indicate that they did not want to suffer the onus of even
people's seeing them accompany their wayward son to
services. The ensuing riot over his speaking, and the
subsequent attempt to cast him to his death from the cliff,
shows what hostility towards Jesus permeated the community.

Jesus later told how his mission was tragically
dividing families between those members who were
enthusiastic about the movement and those who were
unalterably opposed to it. "They shall be divided, father
against son and son against father, mother against daughter
and daughter against mother, mother-in-law against
daughter-in law, and daughter-in-law against her
mother-in-law. . . . And a person's enemies will be those of
his own household" (Luke 12:53; cf. Matthew 10:35-36). When
Jesus made those statements he was likely describing
essentially what had happened in his own home.

The hopelessness of this attempt at reconciliation
probably caused Jesus to leave Nazareth quickly, never to
return. However, Mary's continuing hostile attitude toward
her distinguished son will always remain enshrouded in the
immortal statement he made on that occasion, "A prophet is
not without honor except in his own country, and among his

own relatives, and in his own house" (Mark 6:4). He thereby
was saying that he had received no respect from the people
of Nazareth, from his own relatives, or even from his own
sisters, brothers, and mother.

It appears that after the Nazareth visit Mary never
heard her son again, and a barrier of irreconcilability
prevailed between them. She had lost another golden
opportunity.

4. The Blessed Womb and Breast?

On a later occasion a woman in the multitude shouted,
"Blessed is the womb which bare you, and the breasts which
you did suck." Jesus quickly replied, "Yea rather, blessed
are they who hear the word of God, and keep it" (Luke
11:27-28). By this statement he was saying, at least by
inference, that Mary did not "hear the word of God, and keep
it," and was not a "blessed" woman.

5. Mary at Easter and After

Silence about Mary in the synoptic-gospel reports of
Holy Week in Jerusalem indicates that, during the turmoil of
those days, she was in her Nazareth home, living in
quietness. In all this, she contrasted sharply with the

other Mary, mother of James and John, who had become part of the disciple group, at least during the latter part of Jesus' ministry. This second Mary accompanied her two sons to Jerusalem and was as near to the cross as women presumably could come. She also was one of the three key women-observers of the Easter events (Matthew 20:20; 27:56; Mark 15:40, 47; 16:1; Luke 24:10).

Acts 1:14 shows that Mary and Jesus' brothers finally hastened to Jerusalem after the reports of Calvary and Easter, evidently to see what had happened to their son and brother. James changed his attitude then, became one of the followers, and in time a chief leader of the incipient Church (Acts 12:17; 15:13; 21:18; I Corinthians 15:7; Galatians 2:9, 12; James 1:1; Jude 1). By contrast, it would appear that Mary remained antagonistic and never became attached to the religious movement her first-born son founded and her second-oldest son continued.

What has been outlined here was the real Mary. This was the Mary who was antagonistic to Jesus and all he worked for and envisioned, from the age of twelve to the day of the cross, and even thereafter. According to the Synoptic Gospels and Acts, she was probably the most disappointing woman in the early Christian movement.

II.

Reversal, Revision, and Expansion in the Fourth Gospel

While the three Synoptic Gospels present the true
picture of Mary, the Fourth Gospel disregards facts and
takes undue liberties in revising and recklessly expanding
the Mary figure. Her attitude toward Jesus becomes
completely reversed. All the Synoptic references to
incidents or inferences which show Mary's disrespect for her
teacher son are eliminated from the Fourth Gospel. Instead,
she is made into the admiring mother.

In the Synoptic Gospels Mary and the brothers were
present in Jesus' audience on only one occasion (Mark
3:31-35). He sensed that their purpose was not to hear his
teachings, but that they had come to take him home with them
and stop his ministry, which they considered a disgrace. By
contrast, John's gospel represents the "mother of Jesus" as
having been present in Jesus' ministry from its beginning to
its last day at Golgotha.

The first day is especially revealing, when Mary took
Jesus with her to the marriage feast at Cana of Galilee
(John 2). When the wine gave out she said to him, "They
have no wine," inferring that he should unveil his supposed
miraculous powers by supplying the lack. He demurred,

saying, "My hour has not yet come." She apparently felt
certain that his "hour" had come. To that end she seized
the initiative by requesting the servants to do whatever he
might suggest. Upon second thought, he is shown to conclude
that his mother had the better judgment. He accordingly is
said to have complied by turning some 150-200 gallons of
water in six storage jars into wine (John 2:6). Jonn
concluded by saying, "This beginning of his signs Jesus did
in Cana of Galilee and manifested his glory" (vs. 11). By
this episode in Cana, that gospel makes it apparent that
Mary played the strategic role in launching Jesus on his
ministerial career.

According to John, Jesus' debut at the famed wedding
feast was followed by a triumphal procession from Cana to
Capernaum as the public inauguration of his ministry:
Jesus, followed by Mary, his brothers, and the disciples
(John 2:12).

Although Mary does not receive specific mention again
until in chapter 19, John 2 would suggest the implication
that she always was at his right hand, serving essentially
as his executive secretary. There is such intimacy that the
name Mary is never used in this gospel, but only the
"mother" of Jesus (John 2:1, 3, 5, 12; 6:42; 19:25, 26,
27). The brothers are also portrayed as appreciative,
receptive, and presumably accompanying him throughout his

ministry (John 2:12; 7:3, 5, 10). At least Mary and the
brothers are presented in the Fourth Gospel as always
thoroughly supportive of Jesus and his mission.

In contrast with the Synoptic Gospels, where Mary was
apparently at her Nazareth home in Galilee and therefore not
in Jerusalem when the crucifixion took place, in the Fourth
Gospel she was made to be present. As any good mother
should have done, she is represented at the foot of the
cross, giving her son comfort in his dying hour (John
19:25-27).

The superb relations between Jesus and his mother in
the Fourth Gospel are climaxed at this point by Jesus, in
his dying moments, making provision for his esteemed
mother's future care. He committed her to John in the words
"Woman, behold your son." That is, she is to rely on John
for the future care which Jesus, if he had lived, would have
provided. By saying to John, "Behold your mother" Jesus was
calling upon him to accept this new responsibility (John
19:26-27).

An appended note states that John accepted: "And from
that hour the disciples took her to his own home." Thereby
the Fourth Gospel made Jesus shift responsibility for Mary's
terminal care from her remaining four sons to "the disciple
whom Jesus loved" (John 19:27).

The hostility between Jesus and his mother in the Synoptic Gospels is finally completely neutralized here at the foot of the cross and is transformed into mutual respect and concern. The author of the Fourth Gospel is so interested in this final sacrament of friendship between son and mother that Jesus' suffering on the cross is virtually forgotten. The Mary who was not even present in Jerusalem on that occasion thereby became the Mary who occupied the spotlight of attention at the foot of the cross.

Alterations in the Fourth Gospel stem from the ostensible determination to reconstruct the life of Jesus and the figure of Mary as they should have been rather than as they were. The author of the Fourth Gospel has done a superb job of complete reversal, turning the antagonistic synoptic Mary into the appreciative mother who adored her son. This is a case where laudative fiction is more pleasant than the bitter truth.

A great inadequacy of New Testament scholarship lies in its failure to observe adequately what the author of the Fourth Gospel has done to the Mary figure and what tremendous effects this change has made by way of directing the trends in subsequent church history. By his reversed portrayal of Mary, John has diverted that segment of gospel narrative off on a tangent of adorationism that was destined to move ever farther from the moorings of truth.

III.

Apocryphizing of Mary in the Passion-Easter Gospels

Apocrypha is the term applied to books, usually written

slightly later, that did not get included in a canon of

Scripture. There is an Old Testament Apocrypha which

contains some fourteen books that did not get included in

the Hebrew Scriptures. Similarly, there are scores of

Christian books and fragments that were produced somewhat

later and did not get included in the New Testament. Those

writings have been collected into what is called the

Apocryphal New Testament.[1]

Probably the only authentic elements in the apocryphal

gospels consist in what was derived from the three canonical

Synoptic Gospels. For the most part the apocryphal gospels

went off on all kinds of fanciful tangents so that their

writings have often been regarded as the New Testament gone

wild.

The daring alterations already made in the canonical

Gospel of John, as observed in the preceding chapter, served

as an incentive to the apocryphal writers to carry on the

elaborative work which John had begun. This is how the

departures in John's gospel became the beginning of much

more radical changes that were destined to take place in

transforming, magnifying, and supernaturalizing the role of Mary. She was to become a lady of miracles, not so much performed by herself but as beneficiary of the countless cosmic attestations that were showered upon her.

In the apocryphal passion and Easter gospels, Mary is made to forge ahead to the point that no one else was able to compare with her. Chapters X and XI of the Acts of Pilate ascribe three new roles to her. When Jesus fell under the cross she is represented as placing herself in the spotlight by delivering a lamentation, then swooning, and then following with another lamentation. In certain manuscripts these lamentations are quite extensive. Another of her innovations consisted in searching out Joseph of Arimathea and begging him to go to Pilate and request the body of Jesus. She is also credited with having been present at the entombment and having given an extensive lamentation there.[2]

Although prohibited by the authorities, Mary went every day to the sepulchre to pray during the period of Jesus' entombment. God rendered her invisible so the guards were unable to see her. "God did not suffer them to see her venerable presence." This is found in the Greek Narrative: Discourse of Saint John the Divine Concerning the Falling Asleep of the Holy Mother of God.[3]

The Book of the Resurrection of Christ by Bartholomew
the Apostle ascribes to Mary, Jesus' mother, what was
recorded of Mary Magdalene in John 20:11-18, with
considerable elaboration. Mary was in the garden where her
son had been entombed and was having quite a conversation
with Philogenes, the owner, about the resurrection events.
At that moment Jesus "appeared to them on the chariot of the
Father" and spoke to Mary. After interchanging greetings,
Jesus gave a long address to Mary, who then replied, "If
indeed I am not permitted to touch thee, at least bless my
body in which thou didst deign to dwell."[4]

While Jesus was still seated "on the chariot of the
Cherubim," and "All the heavenly hosts were about him," he
"blessed the body of Mary." Immediately "She went and gave
the message to the apostles, and Peter blessed her, and they
rejoiced." Soon "The heavens were opened and . . . Jesus
went up, and the apostles gazed after him . . . And then,
with Mary, they offered the Eucharist." Thereafter "The
Father sent the Son down into Galilee to console the
apostles and Mary."[5]

After that, Mary became the central figure in much of
the apocryphal material. On the one hand, she negotiated
with the disciples. On the other, she conferred with Jesus.

Seven days before Jesus' ascension, when Mary was with
the apostles, the Gospel of Bartholomew II tells how they

begged her to tell them "how thou didst conceive the
incomprehensible." She demurred on telling them "this
mystery" for she said, "If I should begin to tell you, fire
will issue forth out of my mouth and consume all the
world." After they insisted, she prayed over the matter and
reluctantly consented. Because of the gravity of the
impending story she said, ". . . come thou, Peter the chief,
and sit on my right hand and put thy left hand beneath mine
armpit; and thou, Andrew, do so on my left hand; and thou,
Bartholomew, set thy knees against my back and hold my
shoulders, lest when I begin to speak my bones be loosed one
from another." Thus braced for the ordeal, Mary proceeded
to tell about the annunciation to her in the temple. "And
as she was saying this, fire issued out of her mouth; and
the world was at the point to come to an end: but Jesus
appeared quickly (Lat. 2, and laid his hand upon her mouth)
and said to Mary: Utter not this mystery, or this day my
whole creation will come to an end (Lat. 2, and the flame
from her mouth ceased)."[6]

A Coptic text of The Assumption tells how Mary lived on
in Jerusalem some years after the resurrection as the focus
of Christian attention. "For ten (Rob. fifteen) years after
the resurrection, according to Josephus and Irenaeus(!),
John and Mary lived together at Jerusalem. One day the
Virgin bade John summon Peter and James: and they sat down

before her and she addressed them, reminding them of the
life of Jesus (up to the Ascension and Pentecost)."[7]

These are typical of the apocryphal expansions in
making attributions to Mary at the time of the cross and its
aftermath. It is certain these ascriptions to Mary are
wholly spurious since, according to the Synoptic Gospels and
Acts, she was not even present in Jerusalem when most of
these events supposedly took place. It gives simply another
complex of illustrations as to how the synthetic traditions
about Mary ran wild to the point where the absent one became
well-nigh the commanding figure in the passion story.

IV.

Spectacular Forebodings, Death, and Entombment

One of the most fantastic examples of fictionalizing is
concerned with the death of Mary. Here the apocryphists
enjoyed free range since apparently no information about her
passing nad survived to the apocryphal age. Unembarrassed
by any historical facts, they set themselves to the task of
reconstructing that event with vigor.

The Assumption: Latin Narrative of Pseudo-Melito tells
how her approaching death was announced to her by an angel.
"And lo, an angel shining in a garment of great brightness
stood before her and came forth with words of greeting,
saying: Hail thou blessed of the Lord, receive the greeting
of him that granted salvation to Jacob by his prophets.
Behold, said he, this palm-branch. I have brought it to
thee from the paradise of the Lord, and thou shalt cause it
to be carried before thy bier on the third day when thou
shalt be taken up out of the body."[8]

According to the aforementioned Coptic text of The
Assumption, a vast funeral cortege arrived from Heaven to
participate in the great event. "VII. On the twenty-first
of Tobi Jesus returned, on the chariot of the cherubim, with
thousands of angels, and David the sweet singer. 'We'

besought him to tell that it was his Mother whom he was to take to himself."[9]

In The Discourse of Theodosius Jesus is made to explain to Mary why she could not be taken to Heaven without first having experienced death. "There were thunderings and lightnings. Jesus came on a chariot of light with Moses, David, the prophets, and the righteous kings, and addressed Mary. (There is a refrain to the speech, 'O my beloved Mother, arise, let us go hence'.) Mary spoke comfort to the apostles. Jesus spoke of the necessity of death. If she were translated, 'wicked men will think concerning thee that thou art a power which came down from heaven, and that the dispensation (the Incarnation) took place in appearance'."[10]

The Greek Narrative of the Discourse of Saint John the Divine Concerning the Falling Asleep of the Holy Mother of God relates that all disciples and apostles who were on distant mission fields were brought "upon clouds from the ends of the world." All disciples who had died were raised up from their sepulchres and were brought back to life to participate in that momentous occasion. "13 Andrew the brother of Peter, and Philip, Luke and Simon the Canaanite, and Thaddaeus, which were fallen asleep, were raised up by the Holy Ghost out of their sepulchres; unto whom said the Holy Ghost: Think not that the resurrection is now; but for

this cause are ye risen up out of your graves, that ye may
go to salute for an honor and a wonderful sign for the
mother of your Lord and Savior Jesus Christ: for the day is
come near of her departure and going to abide in heaven."
All these were gathered together at Bethlehem "in a moment
of time."[11]

The Assumption: Latin Narrative of Pseudo-Melito
recounts how the disciple John received his summons to that
gathering. "IV. And behold, suddenly, while Saint John was
preaching at Ephesus, on the Lord's day, at the third hour,
there was a great earthquake, and a cloud raised him up and
took him out of the sight of all and brought him before the
door of the house where Mary was. And he knocked at the
door and straightway went in. . . ." She "took him into the
secret part of the house and showed him her grave-clothes
and that palm of light which she had received from the
angel, and charged him to cause it to be borne before her
bed when she should go to the tomb."[12]

The aforementioned Discourse of Saint John the Divine
relates also how several of the other apostles were ·
summoned. Coming from the period after the ascendancy of
Peter's see, the document has all the apostles flown to Rome
as the assembly point for the trip of that massed apostolic
funeral cortege on the clouds to Bethlehem. Peter is
recorded as having said, "I also was in Rome, and about the

dawn I heard a voice by the Holy Ghost saying unto me: The
mother of thy Lord must depart, for the time is come nigh:
go thou unto Bethlehem to salute her: and lo, a cloud of
light caught me up, and I beheld the rest of the apostles
also coming unto me upon clouds, and a voice saying to me:
Go all of you unto Bethlehem. 19 Paul also answered and
said: I also was abiding in a city not very far off from
Rome; . . . And I heard tne Holy Ghost saying unto me: The
mother of thy Lord leaveth this world to go unto the
heavenly places, . . . but go thou also unto Bethlehem to
salute her. And lo, a cloud of light caught me up and set
me where it did set you also. 20 Thomas also answered and
said: I also had passed through the land of the Indians. .
. . and the son of the king's sister, by name Labdanes, was
about to be sealed (baptized) by me in the palace, and
suddenly the Holy Ghost saith unto me: Thou also, Thomas,
go unto Bethlehem to salute the mother of thy Lord, for she
maketh her removal unto heaven. And a cloud of light caught
me up and set me with you." Mark told how he was brought
from Alexandria; James, from Jerusalem; Matthew, from a
voyage on the sea; and Bartholomew, from Egypt; all seized
similarly by the Holy Ghost and borne to their meeting-place
on clouds of light.[13]

Upon arrival of the apostles at Mary's home in
Bethlehem, a series of spectacular supernatural

demonstrations took place as the heavenly funeral cortege
descended to earth. As soon as the apostles arrived, it is
said that Mary told them to "Cast on incense and pray. And
when they had prayed there came a thunder from heaven and a
terrible sound as of chariots, and lo, a multitude of the
host of angels and powers, and a voice as of the Son of man
was heard, and the Seraphim came round about the house
wherein the holy and spotless mother of God, the virgin,
lay: so that all that were in Bethlehem beheld all the
marvelous sights, and went to Jerusalem and declared all the
wonderful things that were come to pass. 27 And it came to
pass after that sound that the sun and the moon appeared
about the house, and an assembly of the first-begotten
saints came unto the house where the mother of the Lord lay,
for her honour and glory. And I saw also many signs come to
pass, blind receiving sight, deaf hearing, lame walking,
lepers cleansed, and them that were possessed of unclean
spirits healed. And every one that was under any sickness
or disease came and touched the wall where she lay, and
cried: Holy Mary, thou that didst bear Christ our God, have
mercy on us. And forthwith they were cured. 28 And many
multitudes that were dwelling in Jerusalem out of every
country because of a vow, when they heard the signs that
were being done in Bethlehem by means of the Lord's mother,
came unto the place seeking to be healed of divers diseases;

and they obtained health. And there was joy unspeakable on
that day of the multitude of them that were healed, with
them also that beheld, glorifying Christ our God and his
mother. And all Jerusalem returned from Bethlehem, keeping
holiday with singing of psalms and spiritual songs."[14]

By alternating between the so-called Homily of Evodius
on The Assumption and The Discourse of Theodosius one gets
the virtually complete Coptic story of Mary's death. The
former tells how the heavenly burial garments were placed on
Mary and that the virgins who had guarded her in the temple
arrived. "VIII. We all wept, and Peter asked if it was not
possible that Mary should never die, and then if she might
not be left to them for a few days. But the Lord said that
her time was accomplished. IX. The women, and also Mary,
wept, but Jesus consoled her. . . . And he kissed her and
blessed them all, and bade Peter look upon the altar for
heavenly garments which the Father had sent to shroud Mary
in. X. Mary arose and was arrayed in the garments, and
turned to the east and uttered a prayer in the language of
heaven, and then lay down, still facing eastward. Jesus
made us stand for the prayer, and the virgins also who used
to minister in the temple and had come to wait on Mary after
the Passion. . . . XI. The virgins stood about Mary
singing, and Jesus sat by her."[15]

In The Discourse of Theodosius "He (Jesus) bade us
prepare her (Mary) for burial, and gave us three palms from
paradise and three branches of the olive-tree which Noah's
dove brought to Noah, and we laid them on her body."[16]

Returning to the Homily of Evodius, "He (Jesus)
comforted her and said to the apostles: Let us draw outside
for a little while, for Death cannot approach while I am
here. And they went out and he sat on a stone, and looked
up to heaven and groaned and said: I have overcome thee, O
Death, that dwellest in the storehouses of the south. Come,
appear to my virgin mother: but not in a fearful shape. He
appeared, and when she saw him, her soul leaped into the
bosom of her son -- white as snow, and he wrapped it in
garments of fine linen and gave it to Michael."[17]

Following the reactions and remarks of Salome and
David, the entombment procedures are described. "XIV.
Jesus shrouded the body in the heavenly garments, and they
were fastened thereto. He bade the apostles take up the
body, Peter bearing the head and John the feet, and carry it
to a new tomb in the field of Jehoshaphat, and watch it for
three and a half days. . . . XV. Jesus ascended with Mary's
soul in the chariot of the Cherubim."[17]

The Discourse of Theodosius describes her soul's
reception in Heaven. "He went up to heaven and presented

the soul to the Father and the Holy Ghost. And the voice of
the Holy Trinity was heard welcoming the soul."[18]

The anti-Semitism in the Homily of Euvodius is shown in
the following episode wnich it supplies in XV. "We took up
the body, and when we came to the field of Jehoshaphat, the
Jews heard the singing and came out intending to burn the
body. But a wall of fire encompassed us, and they were
blinded: . . ."[19]

According to The Discourse of Theodosius, when the Jews
attacked, "The apostles set down the bier and fled.
Darkness came on tne Jews, and they were blinded and smitten
by their own fire. They cried out for mercy and were
healed, and many were converted."[20]

Theodosius went on to say, "We here encounter the high
priest whose hand is smitten off when he touches the bier:
. . . The high priest begs to be healed. . . . Peter bids
him, if he believes, to embrace the body of the Virgin and
profess his belief. He does so and takes his own cut-off
hand and puts it to the stump, and it adheres. Peter bids
him take 'this palm branch' and go to the city and lay it on
the eyes of those who are blind. He found many of them
lamenting, and all who believed were healed."[21]

The Homily of Evodius resumes by telling how ". . . the
body was laid in the tomb and watched it for three and a
half days. . . . XVII. At mid-day on the fourth day all

were gathered at the tomb. A great voice came, saying: Go every one to his place till the seventh month: for I have hardened the heart of the Jews, and they will not be able to find the tomb or the body . . . XIX. Such was the death of the Virgin on the 21st of Tobi. . . ."[22]

When this apocryphal writer stated that Mary's body was buried in a tomb in the "field of Jehoshaphat,"[23] it is by no means implied that he was thinking of a specific tomb. Since the Valley of Jehoshaphat was the burial place for all Jerusalem people, Mary self-evidently must have been buried there if she died in Jerusalem. The present-day name for this narrow valley is the Kidron Valley. It lies just east of Jerusalem, between that city and the Mount of Olives.

A luxurious tomb, now underground, is pointed out to pilgrims and tourists as Mary's final resting place. It is located on the north side of the Jericho-Jerusalem road, only a few feet from it, as that roadway crosses the Brook Kidron and begins to make its final ascent to the Holy City. One goes down a flight of steps into a spacious tomb chamber with vigil lights surrounding the sarcophagus in which the bodily remains of Mary are supposed to lie. This is the Greek Orthodox tomb of Mary.

Only a stone's throw away, adjoining the Garden of Gethsemane, the Latin Church of the Assumption has been erected over a tomb which the Western Church asserts to have

been the tomb of Mary who subsequently was taken to Heaven.
This is the Roman Catholic tomb of Mary.

The possibility of Mary's having died while on her
post-Easter trip of presumably only a few days to Jerusalem
(Acts 1:14) is remote. If she had died then, it seems the
event would have been mentioned in the early part of Acts.
In the absence of such, the probability is that Mary did not
die in Jerusalem. As Jesus apparently was born not in
Bethlehem but in the family home at Nazareth, Mary likely
did not die in Jerusalem, but also in the same Nazareth home.

This sums up to the conclusion that all the supposed
information regarding the death of Mary, as relayed in this
chapter, is completely fictitious.

V.

The Assumption of Mary to Heaven

In the lore of many peoples, ascension of religious
leaders to Heaven is a rather common phenomenon. Even in
the Bible such dramatic exit from this world is ascribed to
Enoch, Elijah, and Jesus.[24] Intertestament and Rabbinic
literature assert that ten other biblical persons were
privileged to have such miraculous transport to their
heavenly reward.[25] Muslims claim that Muhammad on
horseback ascended to Heaven from Mount Moriah with such
vigor that his followers had to hold on to it or he would
have pulled that holy mountain along with him to Heaven.[26]

In light of all these supposed examples, it would have
been remarkable if the same spectacular transit to Heaven
had not become ascribed to Jesus' mother as she became
increasingly revered. The "Assumption" is the technical
term for this event, the taking of Mary bodily from earth to
Heaven. The apocryphal gospels abound in graphic
descriptions of how and when this cherished event took place.

It is thought that the nucleus of this belief in the
assumption of Mary was begun in Egypt among Coptic circles,
probably late in the third century, and became greatly
elaborated by them during the fourth century. The major

gospel treatises on The Assumption are four in number. They
consist of the Coptic Homily of Evodius, the Coptic
Discourse of Theodosius, the Greek Discourse of Saint John
the Divine Concerning the Falling Asleep of the Holy Mother
of God, and the Latin Narrative of Pseudo-Melito on The
Assumption. In addition there is the Narrative by Joseph of
Arimathaea on The Assumpsion, plus many Syriac
Narratives.[27]

An essential of the aporcyphal view lies in its sharp
dualistic distinction between the "soul" of Mary and the
"body" of Mary. The previous chapter recorded that, at her
death the hosts of Heaven and earth came and transported her
soul to Heaven on the chariot or chariots of the cherubim.
By contrast, it was thought that her body had to be
consigned to the grave for three more days in order that
thereafter she might have an experience of resurrection
comparable to that of Jesus and, like him, ascend to
Heaven. For that event the apocryphists supplied another
cosmic extravaganza as her soul was returned from Heaven on
the "chariot of the cherubim" to be united with her body and
ascend in a new unity to Heaven.

The anti-Semitic Homily of Evodius represents the Jews
as having planned to destroy the tomb of Mary and her body.
He records Jesus' having resorted to preventive measures and
having said, "XVII . . . for I have hardened the heart of

the Jews, and they will not be able to find the tomb or the body till I take it up to heaven." This information was intimated by Jesus to Mary even before her death. She is made to tell "XIX . . . that Jesus had come to her and warned her that her time was accomplished. 'I will hide thy body in the earth, no man shall find it until the day when I raise it incorruptible'."[28]

The Discourse of Theodosius gives a more complete account. "At the third hour of the day the converted high priest came and told Peter that the Jews were still plotting to burn the body and the tomb. Peter warned the disciples: but God sent forgetfulness upon the Jews. And the apostles took courage. And a voice from heaven came also, promising safety."[29]

The most spectacular version of Mary's resurrection, although somewhat brief, is given by the same author. "At the tenth hour there were thunderings, and a choir of angels was heard, and David's harp. Jesus came on the chariots of the Cherubim with the soul of the Virgin seated in his bosom, and greeted us. He called over the coffin and bade the body arise (a long address). IX. The coffin, which been shut like Noah's ark, opened. The body arose and 'embraced its own soul, even as two brothers who are come from a strange country, and they were united one with another'."[30]

Theodosius also has a somewhat variant account. "It came to pass after that we reached the 16th of Mesore, and were gathered with the apostles at the tomb. We saw lightnings and were afraid. There was a sweet odour and a sound of trumpets. The door of the tomb opened: there was a great light within. A chariot descended in fire: Jesus was in it; he greeted us. He called into the tomb: Mary, my mother, arise! And we saw her in the body, as if she had never died. Jesus took her into the chariot. The angels went before them. A voice called, 'Peace be to you, my brethren'. The miracle was even greater than that of the resurrection of Jesus, which no one saw except Mary and Mary Magdalene."[31]

An actual ascension account is found in the Homily of Evodius. "In the seventh month after the death, i.e. on 15th of Mesore, we reassembled at the tomb and spent the night in watching and singing. . . . XVIII. At dawn on the 16th of Mesore, Jesus appeared. Peter said: We are grieved that we have not seen thy Mother since her death. Jesus said: She shall now come. The chariot of the Cherubim appeared with the Virgin seated in it. There were greetings. Jesus . . . spent all that day with us and with his Mother, and gave us the salutation of peace and went up to heaven in glory. XIX. Such was the death of the Virgin on the 21st of Tobi, and her assumption on 16th Mesore. I,

Evodius, saw it all."[32] Evodius was the Bishop of Rome
who succeeded Peter after that apostle presumably was
martyred by Nero in the year 61 or 64.

Another Coptic version, the most simplified and yet
highly miraculous description of The Assumption, got mixed
in with the death account. "When the eyes of the Jews have
been opened: 'there came a great choir of angels and caught
away the body of the Virgin, and Peter and John and we
looked on while she was carried to heaven, until we lost
sight of it."[33]

The Latin Narrative of Pseudo-Melito has ". . . as thou
(Christ) having overcome death dost reign in glory, so thou
shouldest raise up the body of thy mother and take her with
thee rejoicing into heaven. . . . And he (Christ) commanded
Michael the archangel to bring the soul of the holy Mary.
And behold, Michael the archangel rolled away the stone from
the door of the sepulchre, and the Lord said: Rise up, my
love and my kinswoman: thou . . . shalt not suffer
dissolution of the body in the sepulchre. 2 And immediately
Mary rose up from the grave and blessed the Lord, and fell
at the Lord's feet and worshipped him, . . . XVIII. And the
Lord kissed her and departed, and delivered her to the
angels to bear her into paradise. . . . And immediately when
the Lord had so said he was lifted up in a cloud and
received into heaven, and the angels with him, bearing the

blessed Mary into the paradise of God. But the apostles
were taken up upon clouds and returned every one unto the
lot of his preaching, declaring the mighty works of God and
praising the Lord Jesus Christ. . . ."[34]

The Narrative by Joseph of Arimathaea features Thomas
in describing The Assumption. "16 'Then the apostles laid
the body in the tomb with great honour, weeping and singing
for pure love and sweetness. And suddenly a light from
heaven shone round about them, and as they fell to the
earth, the holy body was taken up by angels into heaven'
(the apostles not knowing it). 17 Thomas was suddenly
brought to the Mount of Olives and saw the holy body being
taken up, and cried out to Mary: 'make thy servant glad by
thy mercy, for now thou goest to heaven'. And the girdle
with which the apostles had girt the body was thrown down to
him: he took it and went to the valley of Jehoshaphat. . .
. 20 Then Thomas told them how he had been saying mass in
India (and he still had on his priestly vestments), how he
had been brought to the Mount of Olives and seen the
ascension of Mary and she had given him her girdle: and he
showed it. . . .24 . . .'Whose assumption is this day
reverenced and honoured throughout all the World: . . .'"[35]

The Discourse of St. John the Divine Concerning the
Falling Asleep of the Holy Mother of God states that the

twelve disciples were borne aloft miraculously on twelve clouds, accompanying Mary in her assumption to Heaven. They observed her abode there and the honor accorded her. "And when the third day was fulfilled the voices (of the angels) were no more heard, and thereafter we all perceived that her spotless and precious body was translated into paradise. [Other MSS.: When the apostles went forth from the city of Jerusalem bearing the bed, suddenly twelve clouds of light caught them up, together with the body of our lady, and translated them into paradise.] 49 Now after it was translated, lo, we beheld . . . all the choirs of the saints worshiping the precious body of the mother of the Lord, and we saw a place of light, than which light nothing is brighter, and a great fragrance came from that place whereto her precious and holy body was translated in paradise, and a melody of them that praised him that was born of her: . . . 50 We, therefore, the apostles, when we beheld thus suddenly the translation of her holy body, glorified God who had shown unto us his wonders at the departure of the mother of our Lord Jesus Christ: . . ."[36]

The most dramatic version of the trip of Mary has the apostles transported in a procession to Heaven. This is found in the Syriac Narratives where "Eve, Anna, Elisabeth, Adam, and other patriarchs" were present. Most notable was "the procession of heavenly chariots." By contrast with other accounts where only one chariot usually is mentioned, here there are thirteen, one for Mary and twelve for the disciples. "Twelve chariots took up the apostles and bore them all to Paradise . . . they returned thence and ordained a commemoration of her three times a year."[37]

References to the assumption of Mary may be concluded by showing how it is presented in a contemporary Catholic guidebook to Palestine. "Tomb of the Blessed Virgin. After crossing the Brook of Cedron, the first monument we see on the left at the foot of the Mount of Olives is the Church of the Assumption erected upon the tomb that received the mortal remains of the Blessed Virgin. From this tomb she was taken into heaven, for not being subject to the yoke of sin she bore not the consequences of sin, which are the corruption of the flesh. Therefore, she only went through the tomb but did not delay there; her tomb became the shrine of her glorious Assumption into Heaven."[38]

The foregoing selections, from the imposing array of narratives in the Apocryphal New Testament, indicate that, although belief in The Assumption did not arise until approximately two centuries after Mary's death, it became generally accepted in apocryphal circles by the year 500. Even though certain themes of similarity are common among the documents, the element of variation is notable. Sometimes it seems Mary was taken to Heaven without having experienced death, but usually after having been resurrected following some days or weeks in the tomb. Disagreements in details between the various accounts are the strongest evidence against their authenticity.

It is a tribute to the apostolic Church's devotion to truth that belief in the assumption did not begin to emerge until the late third and fourth centuries, and then only among the Coptic Syriac churches of Egypt and Syria. The canonizers can hardly be credited with excluding assumption materials from the New Testament since most of the apocryphal passion-Easter gospels did not originate until years or centuries after the New Testament canon was closed. The Roman Catholic Church is to be complimented for having looked with suspicion on this doctrine for nineteen centuries.

While the doctrine of the Immaculate Conception of Mary did not become an accepted article of faith until 1854, the doctrine of The Assumption tarried almost a whole century longer. Finally, in 1950 Pope Pius XII "defined" The Assumption of the Blessed Virgin "as a dogma revealed by God that Mary, the immaculate perpetually-virgin Mother of God, after the completion of her earthly life, was assumed body and soul into the glory of heaven."[39] This declaration made the doctrine of The Assumption an official dogma which all Catholics are expected to believe.

How strange that it took the Church nineteen centuries
to discover how Mary made her exit from this life! Only one
item is certain. While the Eastern Orthodox Church observes
The Dormition of the Virgin Mary (the falling asleep of the
Virgin Mary) annually on the fifteenth day of August, in the
Roman Catholic world that day is celebrated as The Feast of
the Assumption, in many countries with great pomp and
fireworks.

VI.

Mary Becomes Mother of God and Queen of Heaven

According to the apocryphists, Mary's arrival in Heaven
was but the beginning of her real vocation as matron of the
celestial regions. If Jesus were God come to earth by way
of an incarnation, then Mary was the "Mother of God." When
the Church came to the point of making the former deduction,
it became virtually forced to make the latter also.
Although the mother-of-God movement gained momentum during
the Middle Ages, it already had become well started in the
apocryphal gospels.

At first there was a bit of timidity in making this
identification, as is expressed in Part I, Recension B of
the Greek Acts of Pilate. "Dysmas, who is struck with the
beauty of Mary and of the child in her arms, adores them,
and says, 'If God had a mother I would have said that thou
art she'."[40] This timidity apparently was caused by the
fear of polytheizing Christianity further, by making another
god out of Mary. Such attribution smacked too much of
primitive religions with their male and female deities,
their sex relations, families, and offspring.

One way of avoiding the dilemmas of polytheizing was to
regard Mary as an angel sent to bear Jesus. To this end the

Book of John the Evangelist has Jesus say, "When my Father thought to send me into the world, he sent his angel before me, by name Mary, to receive me." "He (Nazarius) said that the Blessed Virgin was an angel, and that Christ did not take upon him a human nature but an angelic or heavenly one: . . ."[41]

While this view that Mary was an angel never caught on in the Church, the "mother of God" movement gained increasing popularity with the passing of time. In harmony with that development Mary came to be called "the mother of God" or "the Mother of God."[42] The phrase often appears as "the holy mother of God."[43] Occasionally variant forms are encountered such as the "spotless mother of God,"[44] "their lady the mother of God" or "our lady the mother of God,"[45] "tne mother of the heavenly king."[46] or "the tabernacle of the Most High."[47]

By secondary analogy it thus became possiole for Jesus to be spoken of increasingly as God. Terms used were such as "our God Jesus Christ;"[48] "Verily he is the true God that was born of thee, Mary, mother of God;" "Holy Mary that didst bear Christ wnich is God;" "Christ, even God, that was born of her;" or "Christ our god which was born of her."[49] Accordingly Mary could be addressed as thou "that didst bear Christ our God" and the two could be referred to as "Christ our God and his mother" or simply "God had a

mother" or "God and his Mother."[50] Jesus therefore could
be spoken of as "the Lord God that was born of thee" or
simply "God which was born of her."[51]

This belief that Jesus, of whom Mary was mother, was
really God come down to earth is observed even in his
childhood miracles. For instance, the Gospel of Bartholomew
has, "In your likeness did God form the sparrows, and sent
them forth into the four corners of the world."[52] This
passage refers to the Gospel of Thomas where Jesus at the
age of five made sparrows which "flew and began to cry out
and praise almighty God."[53] This statement means that the
sparrows were praising the five-year-old Jesus, their
creator, whom they knew as God.

The concept of Mary as mother of God got itself
enmeshed in a complex of confused theological involvements.
One such dilemma concerns her time of origin. As the mother
always predates the son, the mother of God must have existed
before God. Since God existed before he created the world,
his mother must have been present at the creation. In
Proverbs 8:22-31 this primeval goddess gives a brilliant
account of the creation as she saw it taking place. Writing
under the name of Wisdom, she describes the glory of that
event in which she participated "as a master workman"
(vs. 30).

Yahweh possessed me in the beginning of his way,

 Before his works of old.

I was in existence from everlasting,

 Before the earth was.

        Proverbs 8:22-23

She then goes on to tell how she had been brought into
existence before the depths, fountains, earth, and vegetation
were brought forth. The achievement of creation is
exultingly described by her.

When he established the heavens, I was there;

 When he set a circle upon the face of the deep;

When he made firm the skies above,

 When the fountains of the deep became strong;

When he gave to the sea its bound,

 That the waters should not transgress his commandment;

When he marked out the foundations of the earth;

 Then I was by him as a master workman,

And I was daily his delight,

 Rejoicing always before him;

Rejoicing in his habitable earth,

 And my delight was with the sons of men.

        Proverbs 8:27-31

As Old Testament time went on, belief in a feminine
associate with God became stronger. She was called the
Queen of Heaven. Jeremiah in particular complained because

". . . the women knead the dough, to make cakes for the
Queen of Heaven" (Jer. 7:18). Apparently in that day the
Israelites in general were accustomed to burn incense to the
"Queen of Heaven, and to pour out drink-offerings to her, as
we have done, we and our fathers, our kings and our princes,
in the cities of Judah and in the streets of Jerusalem"
(Jer. 44:17 cf. vss. 18, 19, 25). In other words, they
observed communion of the bread and wine to the Queen of
Heaven.

When Jeremiah tried to persuade the Jewish refugees in
Egypt to worship Yahweh, they insisted that as long as they
had showered their worship on the Queen of Heaven they ". .
. had plenty of food, and prospered, and experienced no
misfortunes" (Jer. 44:17).

In the polytheistic pantheons of antiquity there
usually was a king or chief of the gods, and also a female
counterpart who was regarded as his wife. This mother
goddess was one of the most important deities in the ancient
Near East. She was called by the various names of Ishtar,
Athtar, Astarte, Ashtoreth, Antit, and Anat. This mother
goddess always was associated with human fertility.[54] In
the course of time Mary was to become identified with this
ancient mother goddess, or perhaps it should be said that
Mary was about to supplant her in certain Christian circles.

Cashing in on these Old Testament and Near Eastern

inheritances, Mary was soon well on her way toward becoming chief executive in the supernal regions, virtual chairperson of the board. However, this development was gradual and did not come into full flower until in medieval times.

Mary was not yet called the "Queen of Heaven" at the time the apocryphal literature was produced. Nevertheless, the groundwork for eventually giving her that designation was implicit in the multitude of elaborate miracles that came to be ascribed to Mary in the apocryphal age.

In The Discourse of Saint John the Divine Concerning the Falling Asleep of the Holy Mother of God it is evident that Mary already had come to be thought of as the great intercessor. "And the Lord abode by her, saying: Behold, henceforth shall thy precious body be translated into paradise, and thine holy soul shall be in the heavens in the treasuries of my Father in surpassing brightness. . . . Every man that calleth upon or entreateth or nameth the name of thine handmaid, grant him thine help. . . . Every soul that calleth upon thy (Mary's) name shall not be put to shame, but shall find mercy and consolation and succour and confidence, both in this world and in that which is to come, before my Father which is in heaven."[55]

The Assumption: Narrative by Joseph of Arimathaea ends with the words, ". . . let us constantly pray her that she remember us before her most merciful son in heaven: . . ."

Manuscript C has a codicil which states ". . . that any Christian who has this writing in his house will be safe from various afflictions -- lunacy, deafness, blindness, sudden death -- and he will have the protection of the Virgin at his end." The lateness of many of these apocryphal views is illustrated by the fact that this Italian document, supposedly by Joseph of Arimathea, is adjudged to be not earlier than the thirteenth century.[56]

As an "advocate" in Heaven to the various members of the "Holy Trinity," Mary became the great processor of petitions. She presumably was thought to decide which should be answered and which should not, together with establishing the urgency of each. In these ways, as Queen of Heaven, she has gradually taken an ever-more strategic role in administering the supernal regions.

By contrast with this "theory" regarding Mary's role as advocate, in which she remains not a part of "deity," in practice she has come to be worshiped, as a fourth member of a quaternary, by the unsophisticated hosts in those segments of the Church which unduly exalt her. For millions of worshipers she has become the most potent being in Heaven, virtually the chief deity of the universe. For a large portion of Christians, Mary the Queen of Heaven and her blessed Son have thus largely replaced even God himself, who finds little place in such circles of worship. This

exclusion has been done under the pretext that God is too
remote to be implored by mortal man. The Holy Ghost has
been the chief victim, almost lost along the way.

This is Mary of the Assumption, Mother of God, Queen of
Heaven, and chief officer in the heavenly court.

The beginning of all this development, if such it may
be called, lies in the New Testament's conceiving of Heaven
as a kingdom. Since the apocryphists spoke of "the King of
glory," "the great king," "the heavenly King," "the King,"
"King of the heavens," "King of the ages," etc.[57] it was
inevitable that the concept of queenship should develop for
where there is a king, there usually is a queen. Since Mary
was the most logical candidate for this position, she was
given the award.

It is an anomaly that belief in Mary as the Queen of
Heaven has achieved its perhaps greatest vogue in the
twentieth century. In images of Mary today she therefore is
not dressed in the simple peasant garb of Nazareth women of
that day, but usually in all the luxury and glory of a
queen. This is Mary of the Assumption, the Mother of God,
the Queen of Heaven, and chief administrator of the heavenly
court.

VII.

The Challenge of Truth

Looking back over the pages of this study, one is forced to conclude that this is one of the most fantastic cases of an about-face in religious history.

The Synoptic Gospels have been seen to indicate that Mary was opposed to all that Jesus said and did from the age of twelve, throughout his ministry, and to the end of her life. There is no evidence that Mary and the brothers were present in any of Jesus' audiences to listen to his teaching. Only once did they appear, and then not to hear what he was saying but to terminate his public work and bring him home. Mary was not present at the crucifixion or on Easter day.

The transformation of Mary from antagonist to her son's greatest admirer was brought about by the author of the Fourth Gospel:

(1) Mary and the brothers were made into devoted followers of Jesus, helpfully accompanying him from the beginning of his ministry to its end.

(2) Mary, Jesus' antagonist, became virtually his attendant secretary and prompter.

(3) The Mary who was not present in Jerusalem on that notable weekend was remade into the Mary who was at the foot of the cross, as any good mother should have been.

Since "believers" tend to follow fancy rather than truth, and since the Fourth Gospel presents the Mary that should have been rather than Mary as she was, this was a key element in making the Fourth Gospel the favorite of the supposed Christian Church.

The Fourth Gospel proved to be a godsend to the theologians of the apocryphal age as they followed its lead in further exalting the figure of Mary, amplifying it in unbelievable manner. It was observed that these reckless commentators began by fictionizing Mary into the most commanding person in the Christian movement. This laudation soon reached the skies as she became transformed into the mother of God, Queen of Heaven, chief executive officer, virtually the most powerful deity in Heaven, and the object of worship. Such was the transformation that placed another deity in the orbit of Heaven. This is a signal example of the snowball-rolling process in theology, the farther from origins the greater the amount of error that is picked up.

This radical departure from truthfulness in unduly elevating Mary was to become a major factor in the meteoric rise of Islam. Having heard apocryphal preaching, Muhammad thought that the Christian trinity was God, Jesus, and his

mother. Revolting against such Christian polytheizing of
religion, Muhammad made the Near East resound with his call
to monotheism: "There is no God but God."

A Christianity that had become polytheistic found
itself unable to compete with the momentum of such strong
monotheism. This confrontation resulted in the virtual
extinction of Christianity from the homelands of the Bible
on two continents, the Asiatic and African. Christianity
accordingly vanished almost completely from its strongholds
in North Africa, Egypt, Palestine, Jordan, Syria, Lebanon,
and Turkey. In all those lands only two small Christian
enclaves remain, the Coptic community in Egypt and the
Maronite residue in Lebanon.

Such mounting departure from truth, as Maryolatry, was
instrumental in causing Christianity to be eliminated from
another important segment of the Christian world. Until
1917 Russia was one of the major Christian nations, with
pilgrimages to Palestine and constructing Russian Orthodox
churches, convents, and monasteries throughout biblical
lands. However, the overburden of superstition, especially
the Maryolatry, caused Christianity to be swept away from
that great land with the revolution. As communism spreads
into other nations, the tendency to eliminate Christiantiy
moves with it.

In all religious history there are few examples where
so much has been made of so little, or less than little,
since Mary was on the negative side and against Jesus in the
days of his ministry. This kind of religion, that is based
on falsehood and fantasy, is the type that sooner or later
is likely to bog down into atheism. By contrast, a
Christianity that is based on the solid facts as found in
Mark and Luke, the two earliest surviving gospels, would
seem to have much greater livelihood of enduring, because of
being built on a solid foundation of truth.

Notes   Part IV

1. Montague R. James, <u>The Apocryphal New Testament</u>,
    Oxford, Clarendon Press, 1924, 584 pp.

2. <u>ibid</u>., pp. 116-117.

3. <u>ibid</u>., p. 201.

4. <u>ibid</u>., p. 183.

5. <u>ibid</u>., pp. 184-185.

6. <u>ibid</u>., pp. 170-172.

7. <u>ibid</u>., p. 197.

8. <u>ibid</u>., p. 210.

9. <u>ibid</u>., p. 195.

10. <u>ibid</u>., pp. 198-199.

11. <u>ibid</u>., pp. 202-203.

12. <u>ibid</u>., p. 211.

13. <u>ibid</u>., pp. 203-204.

14. <u>ibid</u>., pp. 204-205.

15. <u>ibid</u>., p. 195.

16. <u>ibid</u>., p. 199.

17. <u>ibid</u>., p. 196.

18. <u>ibid</u>., p. 199.

19. <u>ibid</u>., p. 196.

20. <u>ibid</u>., p. 199.

21. <u>ibid</u>., p. 200.

22. <u>ibid</u>., pp. 196-197.

23. <u>ibid</u>., pp. 196, 199.

Notes   Part IV (cont'd.)

24.   Genesis 5:21-24; II Kings 2:11; Mark 16:19; Luke
       24:51; Acts 1:9.

25.   James Hastings, ed., Encyclopedia of Religion and
       Ethics, Vol. I, pp. 151-153.

26.   The story as told to pilgrims by guides at the Dome of
       the Rock on Mount Moriah in Jerusalem.

27.   Mortimer James, op. cit., pp. 194-227.

28.   ibid., pp. 196-197.

29.   ibid., p. 200.

30.   ibid., p. 199.

31.   ibid., p. 200.

32.   ibid., p. 197.

33.   ibid., p. 196.

34.   ibid., pp. 215-216.

35.   ibid., pp. 217-218.

36.   ibid., pp. 208-209.

37.   ibid., p. 221.

38.   Fr. Eugene Hoade, O.F.M., Guide to the Holy Land,
       Jerusalem, Franciscan Press, 1946, p. 243.

39.   The Catholic Encyclopedia, The Assumption of Mary,
       vol. I, pp. 971-975.

40.   ibid., p. 117.

41.   ibid., pp. 191, 187.

42.   ibid., pp. 116, 206, 208, 210.

Notes   Part IV (cont'd.)

43.   ibid., pp. 201, 202, 204, 205, 207, 210.

44.   ibid., p. 204.

45.   ibid., pp. 206, 208.

46.   ibid., p. 171.

47.   ibid., p. 170.

48.   ibid., p. 202.

49.   ibid., p. 208.

50.   ibid., pp. 202, 205, 117.

51.   ibid., pp. 203, 206.

52.   ibid., p. 171.

53.   Ibid., pp. 59-60.

54.   Books and encyclopedia articles on "Fertility Cults"
      and "The Mother Goddess."

55.   Montague James, op. cit., pp. 207-208.

56.   ibid., p. 218.

57.   ibid., pp. 133-137, 168-171, 179, 196, 207, 211.